THISTLES AND DOCKS

THISTLES
AND
DOCKS

THE HUMOROUS POETRY
OF
BOB BOLAND

Introduction
by
BRENDAN KENNELLY

MERCIER PRESS

MERCIER PRESS
PO Box 5, 5 French Church Street, Cork
16 Hume Street, Dublin 2

© Joe Boland

ISBN 1 85635 131 9

A CIP record for this book is available from the British Library.

10 9 8 7 6 5 4 3 2 1

Printed in Ireland by Colour Books Ltd.

FOREWORD

Bob Boland's imagination lies at the heart of north Kerry. Its landscape and folklore are all part of the richness of his verse as well as his insight into human nature. Like all the early century poets he was of romantic tradition. Bob came from a very inspired family and his father John Boland was very active in public affairs. His brother Daniel received an MBE from the empire of Britain in 1949 for services rendered particularly in the legal field and during the First World War. He was a descendant of the well-known poet Mícheál Ó Longáin.

Bob had a great love for the poetical works of John Keats. During a visit to England to see his brother Daniel in 1950 he went to visit the home of Keats in Hampstead and read 'Ode to a Nightingale' aloud from Keats' book beneath the tree where Keats first heard the nightingale.

As you read the works of Bob Boland you will find words from all the early century poets. He closely resembled the Scottish poet Robert Burns. With very little of Bob's work ever published, it is my privilege to present you with this beautiful collection of poems which will always be associated with enjoyment and with the beautiful things of this earth. I hope these poems will give pleasure in the reading of them.

JOE BOLAND, POET'S GRANDSON
FARNASTACK

INTRODUCTION

Like all my brothers and sisters, I always called him 'Uncle Bob' though he wasn't my uncle at all, but my father's first cousin. Still, 'Uncle Bob' he was first, last and always. I remember him as a pleasant, amiable, articulate man who was at once witty and dreamy. By quick turns he mused and brooded, chatted and laughed. He came from Farnastack, or 'Farn' as it was known to us. He told stories, spoke poetry beautifully and could make the fiddle say 'Mama' or 'Dada'. He had a Shakespearean forehead and his glasses were balanced wisely yet precariously on what people used to call a Roman nose. The Pope's nose was what he called a cooked chicken's bottom. He was naturally racy but he mixed this bawdy language with an idiom which, I later discovered, derived from English Romantic verse. These two strains – the racy talk of Farnastack and the consciously graceful language of the Romantics – are healthily mingled in his own poetry. He is often that most engaging and rare poet – a mock-Romantic, using a sublime language to address some commonplace or mundane subject, and so shedding a special light, frequently comic, on ordinary things. His 'Diary Poems' show what an extraordinary appreciation he had of country life. Only last week, I had the pleasure of meeting High Court Judge Richard Johnson here in Dublin. I mentioned the poetic correspondence between his father, the distinguished dramatist and District Justice, and Bob Boland. He spoke fascinatingly, and at length about both men. What a civilised age it was when Judge and accused could speak to each other in verse!

Bob Boland is, and will remain, something of a legend. This collection of his poems will add to the already considerable stature of that legend. More importantly it will make available to many people those wise and witty poems which only a privileged few have hitherto enjoyed.

It's the variety of theme, tone and style that helps to make this such an engaging book. Poetry, for Bob Boland, is a way of talking candidly to his friends, writing to people in law and government, expressing ribald memories about his time in hospital, writing verse-letters to his daughter, Chriss, or on behalf of friends, speaking directly to a spud, a cowdung, a snail, a gander, King Puck of Puck Fair, a lavatory. It also means talking to a swallow, a corncrake, a load of hay; or to a pile or a 'po'. Lyrical he is by nature; bawdy and funny he is by his heart's compulsion. The result is a poetry with romatic roots and salacious petals; a poetry full of humour and humanity; a poetry that is, above all, grateful to God for this gift of life in all its beautiful simplicity and astounding complexity.

His poetry is at once dreamy and realistic, sublime and risqué, soaring and gutsy – the work of a man living among, and expressing the language of people whose very earthiness makes them all the more open to heaven's angels and saints. That heavenly earthiness, or earthy heavenliness is the moving, funny world of Bob Boland's poems. This book is called *Thistles and Docks*. A thistle is prickly; a dock-leaf soothes and eases. It's a fitting title for this collection.

Over the years, I have often picked up my own slightly battered gathering of his poems, and read them both silently and aloud. I have always enjoyed them. There's a spirit in them, an intelligent, playful, punning, parodying, mischievous spirit. But this spirit is also warm, humane, beautifully lyrical at moments, deeply comical and, now and then, bordering on the mystical. This book will inspire laughter and tears, it will bring back memories to some, awaken speculative wonder in others. But all, without exception will, I venture to suggest, get deep and lasting pleasure from these poems.

BRENDAN KENNELLY
TRINITY COLLEGE, DUBLIN

ADVENTURES

WITH AN

ENEMA

June 5th   Time – The evening

PART I

RETROSPECTION

Oh, evening fair, beloved thy peace
And holy calm, when labours cease;
When Nature's hush transforms the soul
To beauty, as the mind will roll
Out the broad canvas – Rembrandt-like –
To paint the scenes that inward strike
At such a time – No stain or blot
On thought the tongue can utter not.
And now, too soon, the night fulfils
To veil from view those distant hills
That circle round; I, when at home,
Oft viewed with pleasure when alone
As the setting sun a brief time shone –
Lit those dark valleys there along
Our Kerry hills; revealed each nook
To varied beauty at each look.

Oft, too, I watched at break of day
That beautiful peninsula,
While Brandon, couchant o'er the deep,

16

Seemed to waken, too, from sleep,
And wipe the night mist from his face
That folded him like phantom lace
The nymphs hath woven from the sea
That warps him round eternally.

Oh, I'm as lonely as my song;
Lone as the Prisoner of Chillon;
(Poor Bonnivard, whose footsteps well
Hath worn the stone floor in the cell,
Within that Castle's dungeon there
Lapped by the waves of Leman fair)
Being here hemmed in and not content –
Oh! how the hours bring languishment
To roam once more my native plain
And gaze on those dear scenes again;
Though here's no cavern, dungeon, vault,
But architecture without fault.
Its style each visitor impressed –
Ionic splashed with Romanesque,
With large stone letters there arrayed
Outside beneath its great façade;
No sweeter name could they display
Than 'Mater Misericordiae'.

So, waking from this reverie,
And dreams of home and scenery,
My Muse must take a different bend;
I pray and hope it won't offend.
So, cheerful be the vulgar lay
That tells my 'venture yesterday.

Part II

THE MATRON

The Matron in this sombre place
Is monarch of a 'patient' race.
When I say 'patient' 'tis to bring
Our patience here in suffering
Athwart your ken – not meaning all
As patients in the Hospital.

Before her glance the nurses fly
Like chickens when the hawk is nigh.
She moves around with looks austere
And every nurse those looks revere.
Her haughty import seems to say:
'These are my subjects – all obey!'

And, as she winged her daily round,
From ward to ward I always found
That every patient had his bed
Laid over with a clean white spread;
But when the old rap passed her way
'Twas neatly folded till next day.

This noon-day function in each ward
Was like the changing of the Guard;
But we had no bugle-call or lilt
To trumpet in this 'change of quilt'
But two dear nurses, neat and bright

As is the morning star ere night
Meets dawn, perform willingly
This rather simple ceremony.

Oh, I had so much detested her,
I'd scent her in the corridor.
She made me sick when I was well;
She made me curse and swear like hell;
Oft made me feel in such a state
That I felt my bowels evacuate.

Although I was by nature fated
To be 'bound' and constipated;
All would not do, the very sight
Of old McSweeney made me shite.
Had I a thousand years to live
I'd never need a purgative,
But the presence of McSweeney
Was quicker than 'black-jack' to me.

But I digress. Should I profane
Or to transgress my Muse's flame
By writing in such burlesque style
I beg your pardon all the while.

Part III

THE NURSES

To Nurses all my fond Muse sings
A paean of praise – to them it springs
From a deep source and must flow on
Pure as the fount from Helicon.

I do uphold this whirling sphere
Holds nothing to the heart as dear;
I think their presence can sustain
The latest breath – or sweeten pain;
In heart and soul, all must confess,
Epitome of tenderness.

Within most human hearts there is
A chasm vast – a deep abyss;
A crater, call it, if you care –
I think it is volcanic there
And from within its solitude
The lava of sweet gratitude
Must heave and flow to those dear things
Who tend on human sufferings.

For here, within the hospital,
They're ever at your beck and call,
To hand you 'that', or give you 'this',
The 'bottle' when you want to piss;
When the bowels start on the move –

See! how alert they are to shove
The loving bed-pan underneath
Before you'd shit upon the sheet.

The things they do both day and night
Would surely shock an Anchorite.
Just seen a patient (sick, indeed!)
Up through his arse he got his feed;
I thought it strange, indeed, no doubt,
Denying that pleasure to his mouth.
Who would not see but 'twas misplaced –
No palate or a tongue to taste!

Your pardon, if I'm rude again –
I call a spade a spade, and then
I do not err, as for my part,
'Tis not a Diamond, Club or Heart.
You'll say such things are natural!
Go, then! impute to Eve the 'fall'
That filled this fountain pen of mine
With shit instead of ink to rhyme.

Part IV

ADVENTURE WITH NURSE DOYLE

And shalt thou know how sick was I
On yesterday? 'Twere sweet to die
If only Death would come and cast
Aside this bond of clay at last
And let my spirit go and rise
To 'Home' pre-destined in the skies.

Oh, reader, is this chant of mine
Too optimistic, or divine?
For, as I ponder here tonight,
The enemies I had to fight –
The world, the Devil, I could control,
And flesh likewise, though on my soul,
As now again I contemplate
I oft desired to populate
Against the law, and had to strike
Below the belt to win the fight –
But other torments at me tore
Than those described just heretofore.
Large gastric ulcers were the bane
That made me chew the cud of pain,
For many a day, for years to last,
Until I thought the die was cast.
A large appendix, too, was there
Inside, as long but not as fair
As that external one I hold

Between my legs, of beauteous mould;
(Those who enjoy my rhyming mood
Condem not this similitude!)

So, roll my song, unceasing roll;
The rapture of thy numbers fling;
I have a grand poetic soul,
If 'twere but filtered at the spring.

Hush! Hush!
My surgeon comes, and to Nurse Doyle
He whispers softly for a while;
Then, like a prophet I foresaw,
The hideous role of 'Enema!'

The doctors' faith in every cure
Is keeping flushed the human sewer;
Be that not strange to you or me,
'Tis part of their philosophy!

I've suffered much from introspection;
I've suffered at each damned injection;
I've suffered, too, from modesty –
Thoughts of the abject scenery
Have made me tremble to the soul
When Nurse starts gazing at my 'hole';
(Though 'anus' is the word to twine
The rudish thought – but not the thyme).

At 10pm Nurse Doyle comes on
With a ghastly tube that's two feet long;

And at one end (it could be seen)
'Twas buttered o'er with Vaseline;
And this was done to lubricate
Each moving part; to eliminate
Stern friction's law and so make smooth
The passage of this demon tube.
She raised the clothes; I did not stir,
But let my arse grin out at her,
And were 'it' ever known to smile
'Twould grin at soap and castor-oil.
'Tis Gospel truth what I do say,
I thought the stitches would give way
That held my wound. It gave much pain,
My laughing at each fruitless aim,
As Leslie here serenely tells
How she tried to force his 'Dardanelles'.

A last resort, I said 'Nurse Doyle,
Just leave it to myself for a while.'
To tell the truth, I felt it sore –
Her futile jabs at my back door.
Think to yourself my anguished mood
As I caught the cold and clammy tube.
You know it's only with a 'glass'
That a man can hope to view his 'ass';
But I had none, so had to find
My way to poke it up behind.

Oh! what a perfect sense of touch
To find that 'eye' that saw as much
As Nurse Doyle's 'pair' that couldn't see

E'en when it winked most lovingly.
What plumber could, with neat perfection,
Make such a water-tight connection?

So, in 'motor-language' I'll describe
What next did happen. 'Tis with pride
I will the further tale relate
And vow I shan't expatiate
The subject, lest it should become
A bore to thee – 'tis long begun!

Part V

THE HUMAN AUTO

So, for the pleasure of rhyme,
To satisfy this whim of mine,
As concise as I can explain,
I'll tell you now how I became
What Yankees call an automobile
With Nurse Doyle at my 'steering-wheel'.

Connection made, my spirits sank
As she pumped the juice into my 'tank';
For then I knew that I should be
Soon 'on the road' as speedily
As ever went the shooting star.
Through ether, space or meteor.
I asked then if this juice had been

More powerful than the 'gasoline'.
She replied curt, and said it was
By far a more explosive gas,
And also, too, would give much better
Mixture in my 'carburettor'.
'But, then,' (she added with a smile)
'You'll burn more gallons to the mile!'

She almost pumped to overflowing,
So fussy she to get me going.
She caught my 'Chassis' and, with ease,
She pulled and said; 'Now, sit up please!'
Obesiance made, the rubber sheet
And 'engine-pan' she placed beneath.
As o'er the latter then I bent,
A 'prime', a 'crank', and off I went.

You never saw an easier start;
I blew the horn with a fart;
At which my chauffeur-Nurse inquired
Now what was wrong – had I backfired?

I answered not, my intuition
Premised she thought it 'late ignition'.
Swiftly I blew another fart.
'Oh, cripes!' she said, 'Advance the spark!
And Mr Boland, I'd much prefer
That you would fit a silencer.'

My intermittent firing, so
Much upset her – did she know

Just what to do, or could she see
What in the hell was wrong with me.
My trouble eager to discover
She kept my engine ticking over.

She walked beside me – in a blink
Aloud she screamed: 'Oh, that's the stink!
From your exhaust, 'tis plainly seen
Where all your trouble now has been.
Rich mixture, too, I'm sure would tend
To cause that "knock" in your "big end".'
"Twas rather rich,' said I, 'Nurse Doyle,
For you pumped in too much castor-oil!'

She looked at me excitedly:
'A dekko at your plug?' says she;
'For I am not at all surprised
But that it must be carbonised.'
She caught 'it' gently in her hand
And felt 'it' gradually expand.
She also felt a 'current' flow –
Was it 'electric'? – I don't know
But like a prisoner in the dock
I saw her shudder. Was it shock
That made her seem nor wish to care
If yet 'high tension' still was there.

Now science has taught us, so complete,
How metals all expand with heat;
Indeed her dogmas are so true,
And cold must cause contraction, too.

But has science taught us to understand
How 'sparking plugs' an inch expand
With the soothing heat of a nurse's hand?
'Tis my idea that science has more
And many secrets to explore;
And things will be, I do contend
That science will never comprehend.

I think we had better now assign
Such problems to old Prof. Einstein;
For is he not the ablest Jew
The world has seen or ever knew –
A scientist whose thoughts all lay
Out and beyond the Milky Way,
And comets, born yesterday,
From distant, wombless nebulae
To whirl out beyond the spheres
In orbits of a thousand years
With other suns that set and rise
Outside the gates of Paradise.
Oh reader! he will tell you, these
And less remoter galaxies
Conform to laws that ever live
In that one word called *relative*.
Go meet him then, and he will say:
'Vat can I do for you today?'
Go, tell him how you're mystified
Why sparking plugs are amplified.
Go, tell him of this plug of mine,
Of its expansion, as my rhyme
Has told you in an earlier line.

I hold he'll ope his wondrous eyes
And pierce the vast infinities
Sailing through surfless seas of thought
To solve the question that you brought;
Next pull his eyelids down and pause
To ponder on eternal laws
And lo! his answer sure will be:
"Twas simply – *relativity!'*

Digression's my besetting sin;
My zooming Muse gets into spin,
Wavering often in her flight
To plunge or nose-dive out of sight.

Back to my theme. I have tonight
My further 'ventures to exploit.

'I can't unscrew this plug,' she said,
'For it has tightened in the thread,
And on my soul,' she cursed and swore,
'A stiffer plug ne'er met before.
What make is it?' she asked of me;
'Is it Sphinx or KLG;
Or is it Lodge?' she fondly cried.
"Tis Champion X, Nurse,' I replied.
A splendid plug, I may remark;
"Tis famous for its triple spark.
Experience past to me has shown
I'd better leave the thing alone
For too much fiddling might uncrown
And break its insulation down.

'What "make" are you, I'd like to know?
You have no maker's name to show?'
She looked at me for the reply:
'A one-cylinder Jap,' said I.
'Well, that is strange, upon my word,
I really thought you were a Ford
For "Henry" has that happy mode
Of always kicking on the road.'

So, without causing any pain,
She raised my 'bonnet' up again
And there, at last, tho' much provok'd
She saw it was my jet was choked.
With nimble fingers, deft with care,
She freed it with her pricker there
And got me going. With latent power
I shit at sixty miles an hour!

HOSPITAL REFLECTIONS

BEFORE AND AFTER MY SECOND OPERATION

(Note: After diagnosis my physician informed me that I could die at any minute.)

Hark! There across from Eccles Street
The Berkeley bells are chiming sweet
And for a while the summer breeze
Is filled with their soft cadences –
The passing hours Carilloneur;
Those tongues of brass are telling there
Of time that hurries, oh, how fleet!
Soon I shall part with Him and meet
What mortals here below just call
Eternity, inside whose wall
Time never was or could not steer
His measurements as we do here.

Why do I thus anticipate?
Such morbid thoughts will oft-times break
In on the mind like waves that slake
Upon the beach their tortured foam
And back retreat with sullen moan:
Or like Aurora, when at night
It shoots its intermittent light
In shafts across our Northern skies
In tints that vary as they rise.
Thus will they flash the anguished mind
Nor leave one ray of hope behind,

For tomorrow on the slab I lie,
Prepared to live – prepared to die!
The drowning grasp to cling to life,
This ripping thought – the surgeon's knife!

Be still, my soul, as I repose
For yonder pouch that's for my nose
I shall inhale, then, in a dream
Go floating down oblivion's stream;
This ether which the doctor gave,
So different from that ether wave
That brings along from alien skies
Those lovely choral symphonies
That trance the soul with joy and stay
The torpor of the wearied day.

Music! language sweet of Heaven!
Vibrant nymph, have I not striven
Ever in vain to emulate
The Art by which a bow could make
Thy numbers flow in soulful choir
From violin's depths, like to the lyre
Orpheus played in the long ago
And streams would listen than to flow?

Happy coma! While sleeping there
I'm wheeled out in a trolley-chair
To my own ward – to wake up then
And feel my sore-gashed abdomen
Stitched up as well as had it been
Done by a Singer sewing machine!

ON THE LIFT WITH SISTER JOHN

(The patient had been reading of the 'Conquest of Everest' and awoke from an operational anaesthetic sleep as follows:--)

All thought and feeling gone adrift, Sister John,
As I headed for the lift, Sister John,
For the spectrum in my brain
Revealed to me once again
Those ops with all their pain, Sister John.

I look into your dark brown eyes, Sister John,
'Twas the glimpse of Paradise, Sister John,
Then travelling up, to me did seem
My years were only just nineteen,
I felt the fire of Love's Young Dream, Sister John.

Those eyes that did unceasing roll, Sister John,
And had their orbit round my soul, Sister John,
And so the Lord, at my behest
Runs high this lift to Everest
And we two lone upon its crest, Sister John.

And you'll stay with me always, Sister John,
Among those lovely Himalayas, Sister John,
Love will be our food each day,
No clouds shall zoom our skies to stay;
At night in some ravine we'll pray, Sister John.

And you broke your vows for me, Sister John

Still retaining chastity, Sister John,
High snowy regions such as these
Love's sweet emotions always freeze;
We can but flit like working bees, Sister John.

Your eyes still dazzle as they shine, Sister John,
Not good for this poor soul of mine, Sister John
Yet here our love can ne'er endure
In this grand zero temperature,
We, as the snows beneath, more pure, Sister John.

A blizzard threatens; oh! 'tis true, Sister John;
We must get back to Katmandu, Sister John;
Have I been dreaming? Oh, alas!
And what is this has come to pass?
Sure, 'tis your needle in my a'se, Sister John.

HONEYED WORDS

A Versified Application For Sugar for Bees

Lisselton, Co. Kerry. 1st Nov. 1946.

To/ The Department of Industry & Commerce, Dublin.

Dear Sir, I beg, hereby, to make application
For sugar for bees, whose plight is starvation.
Be generous – you must – for my hives (six in number)
Like Europe, are feeling the pinch of the hunger.
You know how the weather down here militated
Against the good 'workers', who waited and waited
For fine sunny days to go out in the clover
But, vain were their longings and Summer's now over;
This is a thought your Department should cherish;
'Tis urgent … 'tis needed … or my 'colonies' perish!

The Allegory

Early this morning, as a frosty sun beamed
On Honey-Home Palace where the Queens were con-
    vened,
Deputed was I, so without apprehension
I went to attend at their Winter Convention.
The Queens, looking famished, sat high on their thrones
Bodyguarded on each side by two 'civic drones';
In harmony all, they gave out their opinions
That nothing but sugar would save their dominions,

38

When one aged Queen, with tears in her eyes,
Exclaimed: 'Robert Leslie, please write The Supplies;
Dispense with their red-tape and quickly consign
Us plenty of sugar, ere we hunger and pine.
Our emissaries told us how Éire had sent
Tons of sugar to Europe – that vast continent –
What wonder we now much be-hum and be-moan
When charity first, sir, should begin at home!
Explain how our hopes ever dashed by our fears
Relied on the work of our brave volunteers,
But we, Robert Leslie, all humming together
Were constantly beaten, you know, by the weather!'

My God! What has happened? The silence grew deep
As one wearied young civic drone fell off asleep,
When quickly the aged Queen, with half-bated breath,
Called two Volunteers who stung him to death.
'A duty!' cried one Queen; 'Let our laws be obeyed!'
'Murder!' cried another, unabashed, undismayed;
Rising up from her throne, she began to relate;
'Ah! he was my sweetheart. Yes, he was my mate.
I remember the morning of our wedding flight;
His vigour, his passion, his speed like a kite,
When up towards the ether, with wings humming loud
He gave me "the razz" right on top of a cloud.
How memory still lingers on beautiful things –
That rapturous morn knit in conjugal wings;
I read in my youth of the Elysian Fields,
Of marital joy, and the pleasure it yields
But naught could compare with that morning of love
With my brown bonnie bee in the Cloudland above.'

THE QUEEN DESCRIBES HER HONEYMOON IN CLOUDLAND

'Oh, dear loving workers, what wonder I weep
As I gaze on my sweetheart there, dead at my feet;
What sweet recollections now chastely illume
My sorrowful heart – of our gay honeymoon;
The beauties of Cloudland – that tense, amber light
Of the May-morning sun gleaming angelic bright
As we flew 'round the crags of cloud amethyst
And rested on peaks for a while to be kissed.
Heaven, with its stars, was our ceiling above
And Cloudland the floor and bed for our love.
An empyrean haze stretched away like a sea
Seemed as shoreless and vast as the Pacific be;
Blue islands with palms like the Dodecanese
And coral pine groves of enchanting South Seas
Whose frondage swept down tipping each happy wave
And giant cypress, too, as if sighing o'er a grave,
Were miraged the while – the scene would then change
With breath of soft wind to rocky cliff range,
And then, for a moment, re-thrilled as before,
Our thoughts would go back to that classic Greek shore,
As brown bonnie darling so frequently wished
To fly to a cave or a hole in the mist;
How could I refuse the glad wink in his eye?
But, Oh, loving workers, I can't tell you why,
With his red, panting lips, humming softly to me:
"Yes, I am your Juan, and you my Haidee";
Oh, dear noble workers, not a moment relax –

Go, make him a casket of the purest of wax
Then dig him a grave not too deep in the clay
With flowers of the fairest you'll tend it each day;
And, too, you shall mould from some new honeycomb
A plinth that will mark where he'll lie all alone;
Scribe deep at the base this line (with the date):
"Ah, he was my sweetheart. Yes, he was my mate!"'

THE AGED QUEEN LOSES HER TEMPER

The poor aged Queen lost her temper again,
Jumping down from her throne, as if writhing in pain;
'To hell with this nonsense and bull-shit,' said she,
''Tis our hunger, not romance, that's worrying me.'
'We'll stop her romancing,' another Queen muttered,
'Whether sweetheart or mate, the poor chap is scuttered!'
Then a mad, fiery worker crashed down in a dive –
Caught the drone by the balls and threw him out of the
    hive.

ROBERT LESLIE'S PERORATION ERE LEAVING HONEY-HOME PALACE

Listening, absorbed, to the Queen's exhortations,
Expounding the saddest of all supplications,
My heart wrung with pity at their desolate plight
So I bowed to each Highness and told them I'd write.
Said I: 'I'll declaim your work thro' long hours,
Wedding the fruit trees, the shrubs and the flowers,
With that gentle art which we call pollination
While Hymen and Pan abide each celebration,
Then homing, with bags full of nectar for honey
And never a thought 'bout that thing we call money;
I'll tell, too, how often your good name is tainted,
How your sting ain't at all as bad as 'tis painted;
Your faces so handsome, serene and so placid,
Manners so good, though your arse has the acid,
And if many, or all, don't like those "injections"
'Tis your "atom-bum" against robbing your "sections";
And, lastly, I'll tell them the first thing to do
Is to send on the permit for sugar for you.'
While, flapping their wings, humming 'Long may you
    live!'
Two hungry young drones led me out of the hive.

WAR-TIME RATIONING

APPLICATION FOR KEROSENE TO GROW WHEAT

To/The Department of Supplies,
Earlsfort Terrace
Dublin.

Dear Mister Lemass,

This has now come to pass –
Pratt and Shell, who sell 'gas'
Refused just to give
Unto me kerosene
For our big tillage scheme
To grow 'Queen Wilhelmine',
For bread and to live.
No sale in November
Of last year's calendar
Pratt then could not render
The oil I required.
I'm stark idle now –
My tractor and plough –
To feed man, pig and cow,
Till the War has expired.
Yet November hath seen
Me to buy kerosene
For my threshing machine
From the local shop-stall;
I explained this, of course,
With much wisdom and force;

44

I explained – I got hoarse –
But vain was it all.
So, for Éire's dear sake,
Please wind up the tape
All Governments make
With a colour so red;
And at once contravene
If such order has been;
Order me kerosene –
I will give you back bread.
No more need to mention
The said contravention
And thanks for attention
To justice for me;
Our beloved Minister!
I remain now, dear sir,
Truly yours (I aver)
Or yours faithfully.

R. L. Boland.

To: R. L. Boland,
Farnastack.

Re Application for kerosene to grow Queen Wilhelmine
spuds.

Sir,

The Department of Seán Lemass
Was not set up for the farming class.
We would not swap our kerosene
For any blighted tuber Queen.
Good sir, let not your ire arise!
'Tis but our wish to put you wise.
To Doctor Ryan you must unbend;
He is the needy farmer's friend.
Through portals wide, in sylvan glade,
With speed let your request be made.
Perhaps your lofty Muse attend –
Pray let her wear a Grecian bend
And with Hippocratic wile
Provoke the broad bucolic smile –
Say that for child-bed, your fair Queen,
Doth need some Liquid Paraffin.
                                        Seán Leydon,
                                        Secretary.

To/Department of Supplies
Ballsbridge, Dublin.

> I'm favoured by your promptitude;
> Thanks for reply and for your mood.
> You sadly erred; it was not meet
> To mix your spuds up with my wheat.
> You should have known my 'Wilhelmine'
> Is *not* a 'blighted tuber queen';
> A golden grain, that, by nature,
> Well deserves its nomenclature.
> Wait, then, the harvest – thou shall see
> Her sail in Éire's Argosy.
> One glaring ad. has always said:
> 'If you must eat, eat Boland's Bread'.
> It is the best – and from my seed
> One's sure to get the purest breed.
> In Mother Earth so prolific,
> I'll sow this seed, and sow it thick.
> I'll daily watch each embryo,
> To swell, to fatten and to grow;
> Soon Earth, with pregnant harvest ripe,
> At christening Pan will play his pipe.
> 'Tis Doctor Ryan who will be there
> To be her gentle accoucheur
> And, with the aid of kerosene,
> He will deliver Wilhelmine.

'Tis midnight, and my Muse is deep
In boding thought, and sighs for sleep;
A trembling thought in days like these –
She fears the 'foot and mouth disease'
And Doctor Ryan an order make
To have her slaughtered at the stake.

                    R. L. Boland.

A further application to The Department of Supplies, Dublin, for kerosene.

Each month I lose a half-a-crown
In 'phoning up to Dublin Town
To get my Kero. permit down.

You are not prompt when I apply,
My storage tank goes desert dry,
And angry farmers shout and cry:

'Why don't they give you paraffin,
To thresh our haggards here within?
God Knows – we'll never till again!'

When farmers whine, the Banshee's wail
Is music to their painful tale
Of rotting ricks in rain and hail.

I'd rather hear the Mermaid shriek
In Ballybunion for a week
In portent what she means to wreak

48

Than hear a farmer swear and blast
When he can't get his corn thrashed
While my good Fordson stands aghast.

Please pity him … then pity me
Being lashed as in the Third Degree
By Mrs Farmer more than he.

Can your Department yet control
Those wicked wives? With me condole!
Pour *oil* upon my troubled soul.

That I should ere disown
An ever faithful partner thou
Who never left me down.

MY OLD MODEL T. FORD

September 1926

I had a bright vision one day when alone.
All poets are good subjects for vision;
When the old bike was gone as previously known
I should now come to some final decision.

One day thus I thought that a car would be nice
So myself and the Missus got busy;
We sold some old hens for to make up the price
And I bought an old Ford – 'a Tin Lizzie'.

Her attractions for me were her four dandy tyres
She had coils for Com. Roller ignition;
For short circuits galore from her broken down wires
I've made many good Acts of Contrition.

I always felt proud when I sat at her wheel
For her steering was sweet to a driver
And I thank God just now for my luck in the deal
On the day she shot home for a fiver.

'Twas the dear Autumn time when the day and the night
As Astronomers tell us, are equal.

Beale Races came off for the peasants' delight
With grand sports the next day as a sequel.

I took this dear Ford; oh, not one of those crocks
Tho' her hood was all torn in patches;
When the mud spattered up thro' the floor to my socks
I then shouted just 'batten down hatches'.

Yet I loved every nut and old bolt in her frame;
They were loose and contented in clanking
When her engine roared out like a derrick or crane
After ten minutes swearing and cranking.

One headlight she wore and it hung out of scant
You could twist it around like her handle;
A misnomer indeed if you call it a lamp
For its watt power was that of a candle.

How often I did sixty-five to the hour
From The Square in Listowel to Ahafona;
Had Campbell but known of her speed and her power
He'd try her on the beach at Daytona.

I arrived at the sports and I felt rather blue
As the crowd gathered quickly around her
And 'Where did you get her?' shouted up one or two;
'Take her out to the Shannon and drown her!'

Beale has two lovely bars as queenly she sits
On the Shannon – I'd live there for ever
And drink from the one that is held by Bill Fitz,
For the other is owned by the river.

In the former you sip of the best beer and wine
Then crow like a cock with emotion;
In the latter you dip in the billowing brine,
'Tis the junction of River and Ocean.

The evening was perfect with scarcely the wind;
The sun glistened on river and brook
Ere he set in red glory away down behind
The bleak barren shore of the Loop

No sooner he'd sank when the Lighthouse displayed
Its beacon bright o'er the wide ocean far
Then I knelt on the road and I silently prayed
For a light like to that for the ould car.

I kept her a year when she laid down to die
Dishevelled, dismantled, forlorn;
A tear starts to my eye when I now see her lie
With the cows and the calves in my barn.

TENTATIVE ADVERTISEMENTS FOR GARAGE

This Garage is a Hospital
Where we repair and fit
New parts for old if you but call
And drive above the *pit*.

Your car, I know, has *Esso* thirst,
Then pull in there outside;
That 'Tiger' he is fit to burst
For 'Extra' was supplied.

Cars we repaired twelve months or so
Still sing their mileage dream;
To the 'Tiger' call they come and go
Like cattle to a stream.

For *Esso* symbolises power
The world knows what I mean;
That's why we're pumping hour by hour
As tank aft' tank we teem.

If motors had but eyes like men
They'd never pass along
This *Esso* street but wait to ken
My dilly or my song.

Would love to see my face I'm sure
For poets are rare they say;
This poet's mind is *Esso* pure
As the Spirit of his Lay.

This is my verse for you today;
For all who wish to read:
Down here below the pumps there lay
The power that's spelt in speed.

Spare is punctured? Drop it in –
(Old Vulcan's out of date)
Tip Top or Pang all in a bang
Is fitted while you wait.

POETIC ADVERTISEMENTS FOR THE LOCAL DRAMA GROUP, THE HILLSIDE PLAYERS

Sunday 26 February 1950

In this world none can deny
That 'The Stage shall never die'!!
Hence this slogan to attest;
Come see good drama at its best,
For those youthful amateurs
Headlined as 'The Hillside Players',
Will, at famed Lisselton Hall,
Take the stage to thrill you all.
Note full-well – the date is fixed:
Night of Feb. the twenty-sixth,
And Robert Leslie shall compete,
To play the volin with his feet.

5 March 1950

A word to the Wise, sure is always enough,
That's why ye're all coming to the hall at Dromclough!
From the hillsides of Pallas, in numbers galore,
See the Players from the Hillside of bright Knockanore!

Come! Come, you'll be welcome, and so anxious to greet
This group of young talent, where many roads meet.
You'll recount on your gain – how can there be losses –
When drama is good at the famous 'Six-Crosses'.

Sunday 12 March 1950

It was Hamlet instructed his Players how to play!
Our Players from the Hillside could teach Hamlet today!
But this old King is dead – guard his sleep Elsinore! –
While we praise those great actors from gay Knockanore.
From the East toward the West, they are blazing the trail:
A mete'oric course, like a comet's bright tail!
From the slopes of Stack's Mountain where streamlets
    begin,
Come down in your hundreds to the Hall at Kilflynn!
Come up from the valley where Feale sweeps to the sea!
Join the crowds ambling out from the Vale of Tralee.

POETIC JUSTICE

ON BEING SUMMONED FOR NOT CUTTING HEDGE

To: Justice Charles Kenny,
District Court Justice,
The Courthouse,
Ballybunion.

Dear Sir

My absence from Court assumed
To which I am summoned to appear
For hedge uncut, untrimmed or pruned
The winter month of present year
Is due to what the proverb says –
The Master's eye (in truth it stands)
When planting spuds these Springtide days,
Can do more work than both his hands.

Your Honour, too, I wish to add
That long before the Order came
From Council Chambers, cut I had
The hedge along, but did remain
A stretch to which I did consign
A future day, and should resign
To ploughing – more urgent at the time.
If thus I did procrastinate,
Cut was the hedge ere yet too late.

So, in your judgement unconstrained
Please fine me little if I'm blamed;
Could I be present, then my face
Might help you to dismiss the case.

Robert Leslie Boland,
Farnastack House,
Lisselton.

On Receiving 3 Summonses for Wings, Tax and Insurance for my lorry at Castleisland Fair and being unable to attend Court, I sent District Justice Johnson, the District Justice, the following:

Wishing not to offend,
Being too far to attend
Hence by proxy defend
With the Muse (my old friend).
You know that a Lorry
Is a deep source of worry
With Tax and Insurance
And driving endurance;
Wings rusting and breaking;
Lads stealing or taking
Our Tax – could you bate 'em!
From the mirror-bar swinging,
Shouting and singing,
Pulled its bolts through the tin, in
The cab at Listowel,
With not time to repair
Ere going this Big Fair
Where I bought up six calves

And six year-and-a-halves,
Then my awful surprise,
Guard's vigilant eye!
When a Guard sees
Small discrepancies
He's duty to do,
Saying: 'Must summon you!'
Not their fault, in a way;
Neither mine, shall I say?
Shall I dare make excuse
Shelt'ring 'neath the loved Muse,
When you can't see my face
To explain well the case,
Perhaps make the fine small –
Maybe no fine at all.
This last line I withdraw
You knowing well the Law
And a good Justice must
Dispense Justice that's just.
Now, reflecting on this,
May be wrong to dismiss –
Less alone this crude rhyme
Might absolve me this time.

To/R. L. Boland, Esq.

My dear Mr Boland, for your Oliver my Roland,
No requital were sure to look sorry;
We took your excuse with the Wings of the Muse;
(You should also have had wings on your lorry).

No need to explain all the trouble and pain
In keeping a lorry full dight;
But you've got to do it or else you will rue it
For the Guards have the keenest of sight.

So in future beware when you go to the Fair,
With bullocks or barley or hay,
That your lights and your tax, your insurance, your glass
And you Plates and your Wings are OK.

Otherwise the loved Muse may be stretched to excuse
And explain if again the law's broken;
For mind the old saw: 'Hard cases, bad law!'
And here's my last word – let it soak in –

Right into your brain, never lose it again,
No matter how toughened your crust is;
Have your 'bus in repair when you go to the Fair
Or perhaps you'll fall foul of the Justice.

> *29th November 1949.*
> *With compliments,*
> *RDFJ.*

Lines written when Patrick A. Boland was summoned for having unlit rear
lamp on motor cycle and having no driving licence.

To/District Justice,
Listowel District Court.

With swollen tonsils most severe
I do regret I can't appear
To answer Garda's summoned call
Before your Honour in Listowel.

While here in bed I convalesce
This ode may leaven my distress
It was not through inadvertence
I failed renewing my licence.
One weakness mine – I must confess –
I suffer from forgetfulness
And then, of course, these motor bikes
Are e'er inconstant with their lights,
So badly spung, hence vibrate more
And circuit short the wires galore;
The tail-light then that looks behind
Can be in this way most unkind
For to the driver there, unknown,
It could be shorted or be 'blown'.

Good for the soul when one's confessed
The devious ways he has transgressed.
Good, too, in Court, I do uphold
When truth – the whole truth – has been told.

Maybe your Honour now has wished
To have this little case dismissed
For in the law (I know as fact)
There is a First Offender's Act.

District Justice
Askeaton
Co. Limerick

Your Honour
'Twas turbulent 'Maigue' was nasty to me
Came over its banks goin' by road to the sea.
Its yellow flood waters beset me that night
The splash of the spate that fused my headlight,
As a poetess I'm feeble regarding the Muse
But feebler by far when car blows a fuse.
To leave me benighted alone, all alone
On the dark distant highway, far, far from home.
Were I married, Oh! My husband should be
A man who for lights has the 'open Ses-a-me'.

SONNETS

SONNET TO A SPUD

Broadcast by the BBC

King of the menu! Oh why on earth
Was the loved Muse unwilling to consign
One paean to you, dear spud? Of thy new birth
In this old land, I thought some poet divine
(As Shelley, Keats) should dearly tell in rhyme
Thy goodness, laughing tuber, and thy worth.
Hath Homer heard, or even could he see
(But no! his eyes were sightless as thine own)
Thy open vest, when cooked so flour'y,
In epic would he treat of thee alone!
Ah! how a Grecian bard would sing of thee
And I have thought, hath Adam but thee sown
In his loved Eden, Eve would sacrifice
Her sad temptation in that Paradise.

SONNET TO A COW-DUNG

Today it was from a friend, that first I heard
You had a beauty and a homely grace,
Poor cow-dung! Playground of the passing bird
That seeks refreshment, or that loves to trace
A claw-print pattern on your soft dark face.
You hold a rich potential, 'tis averred,
For grass and tillage fields – shall I construe
Bucolic poets of great Rome's ancient day

Mused as I do, trod and smeared the shoe
In pastoral walk beyond the Appian Way,
Yet murmured not, but spoke nice words to you;
Horace or Virgil, in long-forgotten lay;
Cow-dung! All nature greets you with a smile
Your blending essence made our Emerald Isle.

SONNET TO A SNAIL

Thou fatted tenant of the green lawn grass
In beaver coat equipped for evening dress!
Thy restful motion, as I watched thee pass
Into the stony fringe where salads press
The moist earth – night's banquet for Your Highness
To gore, with horned face, the leafy mass.
And shall I dare grudge thee the night's repast,
Poor ebon snail? Or shall I haply deem
Thee symbol of patience in a wo'ld fast?
No! Thou spineless slug – nightmare of a dream;
Emblem of sloth in any mould or cast,
A slimy bastard ever hast thou been
And now I hope when comes this morning light
The thrush will whet thee on his appetite.

SONNET TO A GANDER

Audacious fecund gabbler! The world owes
Thee a great debt for thy paternity.
Father to the bed from which Adam rose
From his first sleep with Eve, we can suppose;
(This may have happened, or it may not be.)
When our tired bodies seek the night's repose
Our pillow the plumage of thy family,
Forget in comfort what thy down bestows?
No, old Sultan, our thanks go out to thee
And thy pure dames, where nature cleanly shows
No eunuch need in thy polygamy!
Mate well, old chap! Joyful as he who sows
The good seed. Mate Well! Augment thy breed.
False – that thy work is but to shit and feed!

SONNET TO KING PUCK

Thou feted monarch of a transient day,
King Puck! By thy royal prerogative
This pageantry – this carnival display:
All enjoy thy charter and homage give
Before thy steepled throne; 'Long may you live!'
This orison echoes through the hills away.
The freedom that was thine along the Reeks
With rutting paramours today is caged,
When bounding like the chamois through the peaks

Or down the cleft ravine, when torrents raged
Listening the thunder the cataract speaks;
(Liberty swapped to be a ruler staged!)
Deluded King! I wished one fetched thee down,
For thy balls fit thee better than a crown!

SONNET TO A LAVATORY

Temple of seclusion! aptly set apart
To house the toilet needs. Repository
Where bodily wants are eased and the heart
Feels restful, too, in thy sweet privacy.
Thou art the throne room of soliloquy
Where each lone patron, with no special art,
Relaxes for expulsion, setting free
Imprisoned waste and the unmuffled fart.

Quiet citadel! Kings and Queens have sate
Within thee, glad to leave their votive gift
(So democratic for their Royal state)
And grateful for kind nature's daily shift.

Who would not hail thee, backward edifice?
Cloister for brief retirement and for peace.

SONNET TO 1939

Written at midnight

Into the charnel of dead years you go
Soon, when the tolling bells of midnight chime
Your final knell – Eternity is thine.
Your days were writ in hate and blood and woe;
Old kingdoms rent – States perish in the line
Of conquest, carnage – in their overthrow
History shall record you 'Wicked Thirty-nine'
As Agamemnon stalks for blood to flow.

Begone! You helot of the years that were,
Begone! While widows weep and children pray
For blessed peace; while orphaned hearts shall ne'er
Forget their sorrow till their heads are grey.
Time's scorpion year! Why ever were you born?
You've ringed another notch on my poor horn!

WILL VIOLET/BRYAN COME?

New Year's Night 1952

Oft do I climb each shining galaxy
When night deepens, and 'Luna' sleeping gone;
('Thought' has no frontiers – as infinity)
What joy innate to wander on and on
Where meteors burn, or, seek the comets home!
Recall that early morn of eternity
When God was in His Heaven all alone
Planning the Stars, Angels, and Man – to be!
Ah! Who could doubt the authorship divine? –
(Tonight – plotting – next celestial flight)
Will Violet come? (Dear kindred soul to mine)
My Pilot to those far realms of light?
Those stellar regions where one ever hears
God's symphonies – the Anthems of His Spheres.

ODES

ODE ON SEEING THE FIRST SWALLOW

April 12th 1947

O welcome, happy bird from distant lands
Who now hath helmed thy unerring flight
Across wide lonely seas and desert sands
Uncompassed on thy wing through storm and night
To thy loved natal home from Afric's strands
As guided by Magi's stars unclouded light.
And as the inner vision now expands
I know thy Pilot was the Infinite
So, as I scan this mad crazed world and wide
Mutely I paused to dwell awhile with thee;
If thou to song unmated and denied
Thou teachest Hope and Love and Liberty!
Beyond thy pathless orbit, too, I strove,
Seeking fond hope – eternity of Love.

ODE ON HEARING THE CORNCRAKE

15th April 1947

From little valley yonder where the brook
Runs by the New Meadow – where April sent
Her first wild vernal blooms with full content
Twin raucous notes like the discordant rook
Jar on the ear – to one whose love is bent
Now in homage to Nature's open book
'Tis harmony. Crake! Thy happy coming!

Was it the sport of Nature in her mirth
Sent thee to trumpet in fair Summer's birth
With thy hoarse throat and mad bee humming
His music of fast wings? Did I assert
Thee musical thou rasper whose strumming
Grates – even on this theme I now devote
To a migrant whose arse-hole's in his throat!

ODE TO A PILE

Advertisement for 'Doan's Ointment' for the above

Vile excrescence at my southern gate
Where tender 'members' arch and ache in pain,
And Nature, forceful, fears to defecate,
Yet must obey the urge, nor long remain.

I sat upon the wet grass last night late
And 'thou' stood sentry when the morning came.
Come soothing, healing 'Doan's' and now assuage
The fever'd anguish, as I feel inclined
To seek some hidden pool and there engage
Its limpid waters just to cool behind
The burning heat – like Aetna's fiery rage;
(In simile naught better can I find;)
And as I close this sonneteering page,
Eve's pearly dews beware – else indisposed
As morning finds thine exit wicket closed.

FOR DEDUCTION

I love to hear the thunder, as it rolls!
The rent and torn and crashing atmosphere,
As if the Planet burst between the Poles
And all the cosmic order disappear.
I hymn this ode to 'thunder' none should hear
(Our flatulent discomfort ere 'it' tolls!)
Thou human Organ! If to thee belongs
A most discordant key of raucous tone,
Incorporated never in our songs,
Yet thou'st music and cadence all thine own.
Thou hast thy private rights – but public wrongs!
For those who pipe should pipe thy tune alone!
Schubert loved thee (not, surely, for thy note,
But sighed relief, composing, as he wrote).

ODE TO A PO

Dedicated to the bedrooms of the world

Loved mother of convention, old as time!
Shrine of our nightly pilgrimage ere sleep!
How often have I pondered, long and deep,
On thee, pale urn; immobile bedroom jeep!
Chamber of music for the feminine,
Who, thy earliest potter, shall I seek?
Thou hast been found in King Tut's ancient tomb
(This mummied monarch, too, should have his leak,
And dared not wet his own sepulchral room).

He was before the Roman or the Greek.
The Chaldees knew thee ere they knew the moon.
Old human vase! For human hemispheres!
Ruth filled thee – with her piss and with her tears!

ODE TO A LOAD OF HAY

As it passed me on the way to market

Trimmed neat! Muffling the noisied rumbling cart,
It passed down the old road of shingled grey,
Swaying, heaving, lumbering to the mart.
Summer's reflex! When its lined swath
Diffused the sweet scent of its new-mown day.
Moon-daisies, too, that mimicked Night's pure heart
Of starry shade, and strewed a Milky Way
Were stretched and withered in that load of hay.
Where now is Pan, loved Deity of Spring:
(Complacent myth! Yet deathless thro' the years)
Did he oft pipe thy blades among, and string
His cloven feet with April's gossamers?
Pleasant fancies this passing wain should bring
As o'er yon hill it slowly disappears –
Load of hay today – tomorrow cow-shit ring!

PORTRAITS

To Violet Nolan, Lisselton

Today I seek the artist's touch
To paint a picture here
Of one dear flower, whose lovely bloom
Is fadeless through the year
No shrill or piercing wintry wind
Can mar the matchless grace
Nor summer's sun nor autumn haze
Take beauty from her face
Enchantment rings the garden where
This lovely flower is set
That from one pure white 'Lily' came
And grew a 'Violet'
But now grown more like to the rose
And with its colour vies
And needs not e'er the tints of 'Dawn'
To win their beauty prize
For such would be a wild excess
Where Heaven has endowed
When Shakespeare could not add a hue
Unto the rainbow'd cloud.

A Man among the Men

Fond mem'ry often takes me back
To when I was a boy,
I'm happy to remember still
One day of perfect joy,
The soft down that hath covered o'er
My rosy cheeks and chin
To steal the razor from Old Dad
My first shave to begin.
What Spartan courage then was mine
I never was so brave
Because we had no 'safetys' then
When I began to shave,
As down I drew the shining blade
Soon felt the freshness, then
I also felt I had become
A 'man' among the 'men',
But if 'twere pleasure in those days
When I was wild and free
How changed things are, for now it is
The hardest task for me.

THE BEGGARMAN

He called on me this afternoon
And sat behind the door
And rested there his jaded feet
From shingled roads were sore,
I looked into his kindly face
I saw his tattered clothes
And, through his shoes, just holding on
I counted all his toes
I gave him lunch, and happ'ly then
He rose, and with a prayer
Upon his lips, in gratitude
For such a goodly fare
Then, from a rack, a good old coat
A pair of boots as well
A pants without a hole or patch
Which long should serve him well,
Two 'loves' I bound in that one deed
Of Christian charity
A love for that poor beggar man
And 'Him' who died for me.

Rural Sounds

Each rural sound about the farm
Is tuneful to my ear,
From roosters' morning loud alarm
To evening's last note clear,
The collie's bark, the moo-ing calf
The thrush who'll sweetly sing
The rustling of the haggard trees
Has melody to bring,
The geese, and ducks, and cackling hen
Have raucous notes, I know
The soaring rook and corncrake
Are raspers in the show,
But yet, to me, there's harmony
In every varied sound.
And as I list, attuned, to each
What pleasure have I found
So, 'tis with gratitude I thank
The God who made it so
To give me such a joy in life
Where e'er I move or go.

FRIENDS OF MY HEARTH

DEDICATION TO NURSE WINNIE D ...

(on presenting a copy of poems to her)

Sister spirit! That which I used have been
I am not now – if, with my growing years
I sigh for past romances, vain the dreams
For a return – sad yearnings with their tears
Of recollection oft the heart now sears.
Life's a moor. I trudge alone, and deem
It a mental holiday in the routine
To dwell on thy sweet charms where all endears.

This old dreamer, happy tonight to feel
His heart o'erflow with joy to dedicate
This unwe'd plot of rhymes, should it appeal
To thee, thou fair one, when nursing late
It may solace the midnight hour and keep
Thee from the 'dumps' when 'crocks' won't sleep.

TO PADDY BROWNE

Some to the charnel-house of Fame
In Death alone go down,
But write not there the living name
Of dear old Paddy Browne.

TO GABRIELLE COSTELLO

Written to Gabrielle Costello at time of tea shortage during the War Emergency of 1939–1946.

Dear 'Gay',

I call thee Gay for Gay thou art
Have you got tea?
If so impart
A good half-pound; oh, what a treat
These harvest days to cut the wheat.

Having got one pound that evening, the following lines were sent:

God Bless thy heart, a heart of gold,
Much dearer than the golden shore
Of beauteous sands that ring and hold
The mirror up to Knockanore.

In Memoriam – Dolly Dowling

(Written on the death of a friend who died in USA and whose remains were brought by air to Shannon Airport to be interred in her native Co. Kerry.)

With silvered wings across the stratosphere,
We brought you home;
We brought you home, and laid your bier
In quiet church where Gale sweeps by
In murmuring threnody.

Naught else shall now disturb our Dolly's rest;
Our Dolly's rest;
The wild flowers you loved will yet be press'd
On the green sod when Spring comes soon
To sweeten your sad tomb.

Your mem'ry shall not quickly pass or fade,
Pass or fade
Into that night of unremembrance where you are laid
Will be our thoughts and pilgrimage each day
As 'Requiescat in Pace' we pray.

LINES WRITTEN FOR MISS PHYLLIS DIGGIN

Lines written for Miss Phyllis Diggin of Ballybunion Co. Kerry in answer to reply to a Matrimonial Advertisement.

Your letter received, of the seventh instant dated;
'Tis hard to reply when one feels so elated;
My future looks brighter – each worry and care
In oblivion now sleeps, so let them rest there.
With fond hope and my face, such a future for me
At the 'Bridewell' a bride ever happy to be.
Of one thing I'm certain (if by now you may guess)
You never hath known of the gifts I possess.
A poetess of culture – I'm an artist 'twould seem;
I write Idylls and Lyrics, Love's Song for a theme.
But I know you're romantic, the same as myself;
You write like a dreamer – not worry for pelf.*
Is your farming dry cattle, or wet, tell me now;
I might know where your teat is but not in a cow!
For regarding this cow, I know nothing, I fear
Less alone that she's milked and she's bulled once a
      year;
That's why she looks bovine, dejected and sad;
Her teats pulled the whole year for one mating she's
      had.
I do just like your weight of over twelve stone
The day is soon coming when I'll scale you alone;
When you lie on my balance 'tis then I'll decide
If weight is found wanting the night I'm your bride.

On reflecting that line in your letter today
When you mentioned, in brief, of hair turning grey;
I thought that your Autumn came in very soon;
Is your Harvest now garnered and sheaved ere its
      bloom?
When Autumn is there, oh, it may be unkind
To say Winter, indeed, can't far be behind.
But this snow on your dome, so coldish and sere
Might descend to your base like an Alpine glacier
And my garden you love and long to have tilled
May not bear the fruit when its seedlings are chilled.
Those vast and broad acres of which you have told
And I now, so poor, with the small patch I hold.
Two hundred! Two hundred! what a grand ranch of
      land
And you'd cover my plot with the palm of your
      hand!
But as sure as there's leather in Granny's old shoe
You'd sooner my 'plot' than the whole of Carnew.

Pelf = money

Written For 'Gus Cremins, GAA (Kerry)

(In reply to a poetic epistle he received from one Kathleen Mulcahy of Swords, Co. Dublin, who fell in love, by proxy, when she saw him play All-Ireland Football in Croke Park, Dublin.)

Kathleen! A name that dearly haunts
Memory's sweet glade, for oft 'twas sung
Above my cot by two old aunts
Who cuddled me when I was young.

When they heard my earliest cry,
Prophetic seemed of things to be;
That's why they sung this lullaby
O'er fretful hours in infancy.

'I'll take you home again, Kathleen!'
Oh! how it lingers through the years,
And though your face I've never seen,
The name alone so much endears.

Oh, yes, my love, perhaps we may,
If fate be kind, to meet full soon;
If you come here on holiday
I can forecast our honeymoon.

We'll build a home down by the sea
Then e'en the world on us frowns
We shan't be jailed for forgery
When we start 'making half-a-crowns'.

The joy they'll give when evening falls!
They'll have your looks; they'll have my feet,
Should they be boys, with little balls
Which they can't kick along the street.

We'll tour the East Coast down around;
See Moore's bright waters, Valley sweet;
We'll buy a 'po' for one fat pound
Wherein our own by then will meet.

Your wish expressed, I send my snap;
Keep it fast while life endures;
I know you'll like and love my 'map';
'Tis my request that I get yours.

'DANNO'

(September 14th 1947. Polo Grounds New York)

Since the first shout: 'Up Gold and Green'
The greatest goalie ever seen
For ten long years the 'sticks' between
Is Danno.

Old Gaels will go; new Gaels succeed,
But history's sporting page will read,
One name – indelible indeed –
'Tis Danno.

That name 'O' Keeffe' all will allow
Is great – but gone! His laurelled brow

Has wiped the surname out for now –
He's only Danno!

From old Tralee to New York Town
He's known to all for his renown;
The 'saves' went up but never down
For Danno.

His eye is like an eagle's there
When standing in the 'goalie's square'
The shooting ball – ah, would it dare
Pass Danno?

Oh, no! For now I'll tell you why,
One might as well begin to try
Slip camel through the needle's eye
As ball past Danno.

From Yankee-land when home he comes,
Let's meet him with the fifes and drums,
The Prince of Gaels he now becomes –
This Danno.

This poem was published in the Sunday Press, *23 Nov. 1952.*

TO THE MEMORY OF A FAMOUS DRAUGHTS-PLAYER

(The late Paul Jones of Ballylongford)

Calm is the tide slow ebbing down the creek,
That oft he watched (when the low sun
At even-tide hath mirrored its retreat
In waterscape and shadow) there, when done
His daily toil – as, calm in sleep,
He passed beyond those sunsets of the deep.
We mourn him now. Great battles lost and won
Across the chequer-board will ever keep
His memory with us, till we later come.
Solved has he that greater problem now –
No concept of our finite minds could bound
That vast thought – and as we fling
Aside his little frailties, must avow
That Paul was honoured by the Greatest King
For the 'many' here below he ever 'crowned'.

On Looking on the Portrait of John A. Costello (An Taoiseach)

(Painted by Leo Whelan, Esq., RHA)

Look on this patient face, to which was given
A touch of the eternal. On him now,
And for our sake, secure and firm is set
The Government: for he is of that line
Whose age lays mighty hands upon its son
And leads him to his morning. From those eyes,
Steady with high solemnities of trust,
He gazes forth to what the future holds –
Yes, o'er Éire's four green fields integrant all.
No fugitive from bleak reality,
He'll face his task, and make the honest light
Sufficient ever and only to his need.
Calm, tender, undismayed – in this great man
Is framed our Nation's guide, and on his brow
The old simplicities of strength are laid.
Not twice in many years shall time so grant
An elder brother such as he … portrayed
In this presentment from the painter's hand.

To Violet Nolan

As all the Yankee poets, I guess,
Are making songs to thee;
Yet here is one who, nevertheless,
Seeks not thy love or soft caress,
Whose only wish is God to bless
Your beauteous self – our Éire's Queen
Through all the years that lie between.

Our last good-bye at Shannon Base
Just as the sun so tenderly
Showed his last beam that lit thy face
To parting glances ere they race
Across the convex world apace,
We watched that Meteor of the skies
Fade to a speck, through tearful eyes.

God in His care full then we knew
Was sure to be thy Guide above
And Flagship Holland's pilots too
Were trusty in that flight with you
And Neptune from old oceans blue
Would ken into the stratosphere
And say: 'A new Star's passing here!'

Columbia hails, while we lament
Thy absence long, yet proudly say
Though Stars to fame on twinkle bent
Cross Hollywood's gay firmament
The brightest one 'twas Éire sent!

When will those Yanks retrieve the debt:
Give back our Venus and our Violet?

IMPROMPTU TO VIOLET

Dear Violet

Just received your smashing letter,
Read it o'er and o'er again;
Thank God now, I'm feeling better,
No more sickness, no more pain.

Ne'er you mentioned of our highlight
Trip through azure em-py-rean,
Through the Heaven's lovely sky-light
Where the Angels sit and dream

Shooting past 'Mars' to 'Uranus'
With a squinting look at Venus,
Watch awhile her beauty famous
And big Jupi. rub his penis.

Onward to the constellations,
View their glory over all,
While I rip you combinations
For the heated shower to fall.

It would help the Irish farmer
For the next Spring crop he grows: –
Would he feel a little warmer

If a drop fell on his nose?

Let me know the hour you're ready
Preen your pliant wings tonight
My wing-span is taut and steady
I am waiting for the flight.

With my stool still cold and idle;
Other things are gone amiss –
Ask Mick Sweeney get his bridle
Lead those Drinkers out to piss.

Otherwise there is no thirsting
There will be Horns down below
From the pressure that is bursting
To the banks to overflow.

And Jim Sweeney will be needed
For another drainage scheme
If my counsel goes unheeded –
Not averted – must have been.

But I am an earthly 'dreamer'
With a grand poetic soul
If short-taken – Christmas streamers
I would use to plug my hole.

Violet! Get your pen a-humming,
Just another verse from thee
It will cheer and keep me strumming
Other rhymes along to thee.

SEQUEL TO VIOLET

Violet! Get thy pen a-humming,
I must have a verse from thee
Just to know which night you're coming
Up the 'Milky Way' with me.

Through this Xmas I've been missing,
My *stool* vacant gave you pain?
While lads drinking, sang – and pissing
Went out – came back – sang again.

Home! Poor Leslie, sad and murky
Lone in bed he had to lie
Could not shit his Christmas turkey
Could not ate it – that was Why!

To the 'House of Nolan'

TO BRYAN

Bryan
Get thy pen a-humming,
I must have a verse from thee
Just to know which night you're coming
Up the Milky Way with me.
You must take me on this highlight
Trip through azure empyrean,
Out through Heaven's lovely sky-light
Where the Angels sit and dream
Shooting past Mars to Uranus
Have a squinting look at Venus;
Pause to see her beauty famous;
Take big Jupi. up between us;
Then onward to the constellations,
View their glory over all
Raising loud our supplication
To the God who made them all.

Bryan
Get thy pen a-humming,
I must have a verse from thee;
It will cheer and keep me strumming
Other rhymes along to thee.

Note: This poem has been variously dedicated to Bryan McMahon, Violet Nolan and Nonie Farrell.

THE TWO WHO POLED OUR LIGHTS

(Seán Henchy and his wee bay mare sleighed 1,500 poles in the Rural Electrification Area, Lisselton, Co. Kerry.)

Each morning as I watched them go
Seán Henchy and his wee bay mare
Down the road to the Cross below
'twas 'Peggy, here' and 'gee up, there',
That's how he spoke to his wee bay mare.

At office there, day's route was laid –
What was the burden of her day,
Those jet long poles that must be sleighed,
Not many near but far away
A heavy burden for her day.

She learned to know the marking 'peg'
How gently to the spot she'd slide
And would not move another leg
Till whippletree with chain untied
Were straddled o'er her panting side.

They shuttled thus – as children play –
O'er field and bog and stony scree
Out gaps and gates and muddy clay
Each black pole tracked its destiny
As Peggy strained at whippletree.

'Quare Times' indeed and 'Tulyar'
Will long and long forgotten be

While Henchy and wee bay mare
Will travel down in history.
With 'Peggy here' and 'gee up, there'
When switched all click down at night
Tales will be told by wood and wold
Of 'Two' who poled our light.

Whippletree = the pivoted bar on cart, plough, etc., to which the traces of the horse are attached.

THE MIND'S EYE

TO A DANDELION

(On turning one down with my Tractor Plough on January 19th 1935. This was at the time of the Government 'Compulsory Tillage' Scheme.)

Poor Dandelion! Ere yet the Spring
To further gild thy burnished brow;
I grieve for thee, sweet new-born thing,
Crushed down beneath my tractor plough.

I vision out the fond embrace
Thou yet wouldst give the honeyed bee;
But as the 'scribe' falls on thy face
Scarred is that vision now to me.

In thy young beauty, blithe and wild,
As all thy gaudy species are
I feel as though a little child
I bashed beneath a motor-car.

No more the warm bright sun to feel
With tasselled petals all aglow;
A golden star – if not as real
As aught, indeed, the Heaven's show.

Small tribute this – I wish that I
Could twine a wreath to add thee fame;
When poets all had skipped thee by
And vulgar men reviled thy name.*

Then joy were mine if this scant mood
Of humble praise could only bring
The classic daisy to a weed
And hail thee fairest flower of Spring!

So, as thou rottest neath the loam
That gently gave thee birth, and sent
Thee out too soon, to bloom alone –
Go, now, and blame the Government!!

*In this locality, the dandelion is rudely knows as 'the piss-a-bed'.

THE SNOWMAN
(A figurative sketch, January 1944)

A Stoic that stared from soft and puddled eyes,
With hands outstretched as if to praise or bless
The art that wrought him and moulded his huge size,
A glacial giant, of Arctic frigidness.

Large was the pipe he smoked, of faggot made;
His comforts revelled in the frosty wind;
His cynic smile when leaden clouds hath laid
Another blanket for his feet to bind.

And joyous children came to shout and scream,
Round his broad base, and named him Santa Claus;
But more like Ozymandias did he seem –
Cold and stern, immutable to thaws.

Soon came the moist breath of the warm South
Kissing his icy cheek and brow unstained;
Fear struck the faggot pipe from out his mouth;
He vanished overnight – his pipe remained!

A Schoolboy's Poem to a Bumble Bee

Today I saw a bumble bee
Buzzing through the air with glee.
He was like an aeroplane
Flying through the mist and rain;
By his humming I could tell
God did make his engines well.
He did not need the Gasolene!
He would prefer a bright sunbeam
To light him on his lonely way
On this dark October day.
Now I wonder where he went –
Where his winter will be spent?
He cannot have a fire like me
And will be cold – poor bumble bee!
But then I know One will preside
To watch with him and be his Guide!
To some cosy bower he will go,
Sleep through winter's frost and snow;
Pleasant dreams that sleep will bring
Bright with hopes of sunny Spring
When fluted cup of daffodil

And the lemoned primrose fill
Nature's chequered patterns there
By brake and green field everywhere.
Waits a balmy morn to rise
With the skylark to the skies
(Oh, what joy that day will bring
To hear again his droning wing?)
Sighs for Summer when she calls
Him to the foxglove thimbled halls
Where awhile he'll rest and dine
Sipping nectar for his wine.
Like a sovereign free to rule
With no worries as to school
With no task or book to read,
Master, mistress, to impede.
Mitching days can never enter
In his cerebral centre;
Grinds for honours or for passes;
Fears not Euclid's 'Bridge of Asses'
Algebra or mensuration
Far beneath his sweet creation.
Irish? No! Nor geography! –
I'd love to be a bumble bee.

SPRING DAWN
Killarney April 10th 1947

I stand beside the gateway of the dawn
While yet Aurora murmurs in her sleep
Disturb her slumbers, not awhile, in the lawn
Is peace while cattle browse, but the fawn
Get restless in those yonder copses deep.
Now watch! From curtained couch she has with-
      drawn
Her pleated rainment of soft gold and sheep
Through woolly eyes gaze east as trotters leap.
Quick as the formed bow, in raindrops bright
She's draped o'er earth with owlet wings,
She flies with her soft, tender, loving light;
The worm from his dust-hole creeps, bird hymns
Are luted to the listening Heaven – God
With Mary are blessing the new-turned sod.

CAUGHT

Citing 'Immortal Bird of Night' by Keats:
'Away! Away! For I will fly to thee
Not charioted by Bacchus and his pards'
And then the 'knocker' with its ominous beats
Disturbing, rang the presence of the 'Guards'.

I was the culprit – sorrowed and ashamed
I stood outside the bar and gently gave my name,
I knew I was the one who should be blamed
Being disobedient when the order came.

'Twere my entreaties to Miss Nolan there
To stay her order for a little while
Old moths can too be often caught by glare
For the Guinness it was sweetened by her smile.

TO MY BROOK

May 1st, 1947

Little river, whither going?
Can'st thou not delay?
Ever hurrying, ever flowing,
Through the night and day.
Never weary, never resting,
Crooning up to robins nesting
Along thy mossy way.

113

'Tis a perfect joy to watch thee;
Hear the music thou dost play;
See the shades of light
That catch the
Hurrying bubbles, thither darting,
Some are kissing, some are parting,
Onward in a fray.

He who called thee from thy source
Up in far-off mountain glen;
He who gave thee gentle force
He will bear me on, and then,
I will, one day, like to thee
Join the everlasting sea,
Never to return again.

LONELINESS

Composed, after midnight, whilst walking over a three-mile stretch of moor-land between Ballylongford and Farnastack, Lisselton, County Kerry.

Lone as a ruin in a churchyard, where
The trees are not, but the dead are there!
Lone as a climber on some Alpine peak!
Lone as the last kiss on a lover's cheek!
Lone as a lighthouse on some rocky shore!
Lone as a 'sick' man at a shit-house door!
Lone as the Pole Star from its sky-tower watching!
Lone as a gander when the geese are hatching!
Lone as a maiden, weeping in distress!

Lone as a bullock when the cow says 'Yes!'
Lone as a 'winkle in his twisted shell!
Lone as a Spirit in a hole in Hell!
Lone as a skylark who has lost his song!
Lone as a eunuch, when his 'gems' are gone!
Lone as a shipwreck on the ocean tossed!
Lone as a miser when his hoard is lost!
Lone as a petrel on the stormy wave!
Lone as a dead man in a nameless grave!
Lone as a fat snail in the dewy grass!
Lone as a pimple on an old hag's a'se!
Lone as a night-wind o'er the silent moor!
Lone as a strumpet or a waiting w——e!
Lone as a lassie on the 'bathroom bowl'
When she finds no paper in the toilet-roll!
Lone as the Arctic when the Polar Bear
Howls to the blizzard from his frozen lair!
Lone as a whaler in the ice-pack jammed!
Lone as a jackass when his 'nuts' are clammed!
Lone as the dying rose's scented breath!
Lone! Lone! Lone! e'en itself as Death!

SUNSET

(written on the rocks in Ballybunion)

I've watched the gilt of evening in the skies
When Sol played hide and seek between each cloud
And made the west a golden paradise
Of colour, and all earth seemed bowed
In adoration t' Him who painted there
This beauty chaste from flume* of mist and light;
And my rapt soul following then in prayer –
Until down dropped the curtain of the night.

* *Channel, ravine, trough.*

THE SONG OF THE TRYST

BROWN AND MAGEEN

(Published in The Kerryman *of May 5th, 1934)*
(Air: 'The Mountains O'Mourne')

Winter nights long ago, how often I strode,
To a dear little cabin a mile o'er the road,
Where Life passed as happy as Love's airy dreams
With mirth and with laughter, inside at Mageen's.
A neat little kitchen, with a shop there as cute
Hugged close in a corner like a telephone booth
Where she sold fags and matches, a choice blend of teas,
Soap, candles and pepper and other sundries.

A dresser stood near it and glittered with delph
Which Mage used to boast were as old as herself;
The lustre mugs up there that shone in a row
With jam-pots and dishes and cups to and fro.
A pile of bread-boxes was ranged by the wall
And those were the seats that made comfort for all
And an old sugawn chair that cost just half-a-crown
Long years before Mage hath become Mrs Brown.

In here was the Tryst where the long winter night
Flew swift with the gusts of argument bright;
Here conventions were flouted as well might have been
In this old humble cabin with Brown and Mageen.
Brown's face so good-humoured, as broad as his mind
That never could see but the good in mankind;
Though a large corporation his contour hath spoiled

And it heaved like a billow if only he smiled.

The Rabara Lynch was the first to present
His Bills for the night in this strange Parliament.
He was the loud-speaker though Brown held the Chair
So he spoke from the Benches of bread-boxes there.
As an orator bold, I must frankly admit,
He was fluent and as powerful as Grattan or Pitt;
His speech flowed like a torrent or a mountain cascade
When debating that topic: 'How Roads Should Be Made.'

Books he wrote on this subject some ten years ago;
Their copyright sold to MacAlpine & Co;
Though his Treatise on Quarries, 'The Keystone and Wall
Of Underground Strata' was best of them all.
He was Knight of the Road in his Stewardship one time;
His office was noble – we'll call it sublime;
Who would dare now refute, when all say with one
        mind,
'Twas a loss to his Section the day he resigned.

The cabin's still there, and I now heave a sigh,
To see Mage bending out with the years rolling by;
And old Sebby Brown, too, from senile decay
Just counting his beads and preparing the way;
And this old trysting-place where no longer is heard
The sweeping invective my soul often stirred –
Oh! alas for the joys that were ours in that time –
When Youth had its morning and care was not mine.

THE SEQUEL
(OR BROWN'S WAKE)

This morn, as yet the pale star beams remain,
Poor Brown closed his eyes to this world of pain;
Today, now, I mourn the friend I held dear
As in sorrow I stand by the side of his bier.

I grasped his big hand and the dear nights of old
Came back and I wept when I felt it now cold;
And the pulse of that heart there stilled evermore –
Ticked out its last beat with the weight of fourscore.

The neighbours filed past where he now lay in state,
And the egg-boxes 'round made the seats for the wake;
The shop there – unshuttered – was watched carefully
Lest mourners should pilfer the fags or the tea.

Some came to drink Guinness, Mage would not buy,
But like Érin she stood, with the tear in her eye,
And intuitively scanned down faces that read
Greater thirst for a pint than grief for the dead.

Who is he that now cometh? Oh, gently make way –
'Tis Rabara Lynch, his last tribute to pay.
He brings a wild wreath of the heathers that bloom
Near his own mountain home, to lay on the tomb.

When the old sugawn chair in the corner he spied,
Hear his wit, in his grief, when he said: 'Unemployed!'

There, vacant and idle, its tenant lying low,
Recalled happy dreams of the nights long ago.

Ah yes, we have known him for years now, and hence
No one would have doubted his grief so intense.
An usher then proffered him snuff from a spoon;
He prayed as he sniffed it and made for the room.

Here, bent o'er the corpse, in the silence so deep,
He fingered the 'habit' and knew it was cheap.
With the voice of a stentor*, he uttered aloud –
'Three days!!! and he'll push out his a'se thro' that
    shroud.'

And there through the valley the fast Gale is flowing:
Nearby is the churchyard with wild grasses blowing;
There poor Brown is sleeping – ere his grave will be
    green
She'll be soon called to slumber beside him – Mageen.

Oh, wirra strue**, like a ship tempest tossed,
Or a ship in a tempest when rudder is lost,
Old Mageen drifts on like a wreck to the shore
To be beached by the side of her consort once more.

*Name of a Greek herald in the Trojan War; any person with an unusually powerful voice.

**From the Irish 'A Mhuire is Trua'.

HEAR YE!

LADY DAISY

With little thinking now I've found
Ideas which you'll agree are sound,
In describing this greyhound
Lady Daisy.

Her palmy days are coming on,
When she shall fly, some greyhounds can;
At least so thinks my Uncle Dan,
For he's crazy.

Since the day that first he got her,
Sure you dare look crooked at her,
If perchance you called her flapper,
Oh 'tis then

You'd see his right leg skyward shoot,
And the impetus of his boot
Would be felt where you'd acutely
Feel the pain.

Now having fed her up on steak,
The Venus of her kind, she'll make
Her debut. First racing date,
In County Clare.

Her bright career so soon begun,
She's on the road. The morning sun
Reflects the smile of Maurice Gunn,

Her trainer there.

Now they're on the coursing ground.
You can hear them cheer all round,
As Miss Daisy with a bound
Flies from slips.

But alas she's losing pace;
Watch the nose on Gunny's face,
See 'tis pointing to the place
Where she trips.

Away from Toonach's coursing plain,
Until Kerry's shore they gain,
Filled with chagrin and with pain
They land in Lyre.

Where night's topics soon begin;
How poor Daisy got the spin.
'Twas such, they say within
Around the fire.

But Dan to this would not agree.
He said the hare she could not see.
Then of course she got her pee,
As dogs do.

But she sha'n't so naughty be
When next I'll take her to Tralee.
Ah! she'll win it easily,
The Waterloo.

Now perhaps their bragging's done.
They're lick alike – himself and Gunn.
When next he'll try a better one,
Let us hope

That fortune then will favour him
With speed and power and grit to win.
But, that the morrow will see him swing
The Daisy from a rope.

YOUR VERSIFIED PROGRAMME FOR BALLYBUNION RACE DAY

27th June 1944

Ballybunion all en-fete with Flags and Bunting gay
Extends a hearty welcome when you come to Racing
    Day;
Come on by Bike, by 'Bus, or Hike, with many Pals
    along,
Make best the way this gala day of Sport, of Dance and
    Song;
First, have a splendid surf bath on the silvered shining
    sea,
Next link yourself to Golfland, 'twill suit you to a Tee;
Then lunch in at The Castle or The Central if you care,
Or turn in to Bridie for a good Imperial fare;
Don't forget The Ocean for a decent fine Hotel
And cross the street awhile to meet our Harty Gabrielle,

I'm telling you she holds there too some rare old vintage
   Wines,
For the Skippers of the Clippers who are come here from
   Foynes.
If to Exchange your thoughts should range, drop in to P.J.
   Dee
And finish up the forenoon with a Glass from Michael G,
His Railway Bar the one Bright Star
In our Guinness Galaxy.
But other constellations much like the Milky Way,
Up and down our dear old town keep shining through
   the day;
'Tis a glorious sight to see their light
Reflected on a Tray.
Go northwards to the Paddock in the early afternoon;
To a Grand Stand seat that's hard to beat the towering
   Cliffs of Doon
Have a Green Back on the best horse and when your Bet
   is laid
Just watch him pass the winning post our Clarke will see
   you paid.
I'll wait awhile to snap your smile, so glad to see you
   win;
The deafening cheer when all will hear you say 'I'm
   lucky Jim'
Your evening to Pat Crowley, on the great Pavilion floor,
Its polished Maple sure can woo the gentle Terpsichore;
And oh, his Band, sublimely grand, to hear it echo o'er
Where Cliffs repeat the rhythm beat
Along our golden shore.
When Soldier's Song tells the gay throng

The hour for home and rest, let all rename this town of
    fame
The Venice of the West!

Terpsichore = Muse of Dancing

LETTERS TO MY DAUGHTER

Dear Chriss,

I now must drop to you a line
To wish you happy Xmas time
Full of good things and all good cheer
And happiness in the New Year.
Our stall done up (which was a boon)
Is now more like a 'drawing room'
When cows come in to eat their hay
Then lie and chew all through the day.
Behind them runs a trolley line
To clean them out in rapid time
A pleasant job for any man
But only loved by brother Dan,
Who lives among the cattle there
Tending, feeding, with great care.
Of many things that I would wish
'Tis turkey for your Xmas dish
I hope your hungry Nuns at least
Will treat you to a famous feast
When New Year comes you will not feel
The time go by, as quickly steal
The months away and from the bane
Of nursing crocks be home again.
So, now, once more I must renew
Best Xmas wishes unto you.

From Daddy.

To:
Chrissie on receiving Pull-over

I

Yes! Éire is a fairy Isle
Whose poets have sung her melodies:–
An ocean Queen that could beguile
Like 'Helen' of the Hellenese

II

Killarney, too – each placid lake
Has Isles of crystal purity;
A chain of pearls that surely make
Her 'Home of Beauty' e'er to be.

III

Lough Gill made famous by our Yeats,
Whose soul in sweet captivity
Was held in bondage by the fates
That spell-bound him in 'Innisfree'

IV

And then we have those Coral Isles,
Elysiums of the tropic seas
Where Angels come to rest bewhiles
Beneath their Palms in tapestries

V

Each Isle has its own charm content,
Enduring ever to enthral;
But the Fair Isle P.O. which you sent
Is the dearest Isle of all

VI

So Chrissie dear, though we apart,
This ode in thanks must prove
There is a Fair Isle in your heart
Which holds a Daddy's love.

Dad.

P.S. You read Yeats' 'Fair Isle of Innisfree' the very best of
his poems?

Farnastack
Liselton,
22–12–'53

My Dear Chriss

I take up my pen on this sad Xmas time:–
My Epistle goes forth not in prose but in rhyme,
I send out my wishes so wholly sincere
For a bright happy Xmas and a jolly New Year.
Poetic the mood now with 'thought' running swift
To hail and to thank thee for wonderful gift.
Oh yes! how it fits me, like a glove on the hand
The comment from all was: 'the fitting was grand'

When all had agreed so perfect the fitting,
Said I: 'what brain so intuitive in knitting'.
Now for the new: while the 'Esso' keeps on –
First on the agenda is: Liam has come home.
He's looking quite well, his stomach is fine
Can whack down 'cast iron' when sits down to dine
Best test of all, sure 'twill bring us relief
When he's chucking down Jer'miah's cast iron beef
He says: this he can do with impunity
Rolling down his gullet with avidity.
But in the hall sure it puts my brain reeling
With turkey and geese – this arse to the ceiling
Think of the menu, what sweet thoughts are forming
Blood of the goose going down in the morning.
Oh how I'll smile when it comes up all steaming
My face like the sun in the morning all beaming;
I'll say no more – might it make your mouth water?
And you cannot have some, my dear loving daugh-
      ter.
We 'ave an altar to Mary – ever so dear –
A 'candle' each day for her Marian year.
'Tis lit every night in window before her
Rosary then, though we cannot adore her.
That is for her *Son*, but She will ask for us
Blessings we need for the e'er coming morrows
To cheer, wipe away our tears and our sorrows
Remember I wrote of this sad Xmas time
'Twas sadness to me when I started to rhyme
As I know dear Chriss, my grief you will share,
When at Xmas we see that one vacant chair,
And that old grey ruin near the creek in Saleen

'Neath its shadow down there poor Val's grave is
    green.
The tides come and go, disturb not his sleeping;
God in his Heaven his dear soul is keeping
Ask him back we would not! Surely oh never!
His accordion clasped and silent for ever.
I know as you read you're certain to chide me
As down by this page the tears fall beside me
I'll go off to bed now and shut down mine eyes
'Twill seal up the fountain as old Daddie cries.
And once again Chrissie, my heart opens wide
To renew fondest wishes for a grand Xmas-tide.

Dad.

Farn,
2–6–'55,

Dear Chriss,

I know dearest Chriss that it is now nearly time
To reply to your letter, it goes off in rhyme,
There's not much news from home – all the same whirl
    gig
But your Mammie of course grows as fat as a pig.
Sure the cows have great milk – over 80 a day
Makes the cheques fairly large when the time comes to
    pay,
But we lost it that day in that fast Dublin trip

Put the blame down on Attie – don't blame me a bit!
If he rose when I called him, in early we'd be
Our appointment was 'two' and we landed at three.
We could not have a meal only rushing for time
We just caught our man – bought a trailer sublime.
Your 'Martin' on Friday is bringing it down
In his great mighty lorry as big as a town
Later on I'll go with him and seek Ballyowen
Where the fields are as green as our meadows at home.
I will write you a letter to tell you the day
In Dublin that night with Matt Mulvihill I'll stay.
We have 12 fatted bantams coming on very well
The milk from the 'Traveller' each day makes them swell
On the day of their sale I will go in a 'booze'
I will sing through the day – I will rhyme with the Muse
Tomorrow, at noon we'll be switched on for light*
Imagine your Mammie when she reads now at night
One hundred candle power lamp – what a glorious beam
The kitchen at night, like the day it will seem.
'Twas Shaun did the wiring, Liam did help him one day
We fed them like champions and they looked not for pay.
Well Chriss 'tis my legs that have gone very tired
Would it cure if I rest them or else get them *fired*
Moss Farrell's wife died on last Saturday eve
She was up on the seventy they say – I believe!
She went rather sudden – just in bed for a day
Got this pain round the chest and at eve passed away.
Now most amiable daughter, oh most amiable Chriss
I'm expecting a mighty long letter for this
A line of great news sure I have now for thee
Shaun drives Mum tomorrow for a coat to Tralee.

135

So now Chriss goodbye till I hear from you soon
Ere the days go much farther in this lovely June.

Dad.

Rural Electrification Scheme concluded.

TOWARDS THE HORIZON

Sunday 24th January, 1954

This is the Sabbath day and so to Mass
Home to a goose – what repast could surpass?
Read the Sunday papers relaxing there
Intermittent snooze in kitchen arm-chair.
A day of heavy cloud and driving rain
Which really seems to soothe a tired brain.
At eve I drive with Att to Ballyduff
As sailors say, the night was rather rough!
Heavily down the mighty torrents came;
Clouds were debauched to vomit out again.
At Brown's we spoke above foaming jars
Home at midnight – dreamt of wind, rain and stars.

Monday 25th January, 1954

I rose at eight – just as the sun would rise
Slow and deliberate with Guinnessed eyes;
I walked o'er to the window – looking through
I thought that all the world was washed anew.
A thrush out in the orchard tried to sing
Just a few notes of calling to the Spring;
Perhaps a salutation to its mate
To woo and coo that Spring is at the gate?
Some flags within the stall we just begin;
Eight in calf heifers must be now put in,
And so just passes off another day
The clouds are gone and frost is on the way.

TUESDAY 26TH JANUARY, 1954

Moving higher up the meridian
The longer day we just begin to scan;
The frost has come the fields are covered o'er;
A shadowy thaw and all the morning hoar
Quickly melts; like the beauty that must fade –
As butterfly his golden hour in sunny glade –
This is a day the 'Esso' swift would flow,
Out to the field 'Gafsa'* spreading go.
Asdee has lost another lovely son
A dear Walsh boy killed in Albion
Tonight his body sadly comes to home
Tomorrow resting with the dead alone.

*Gafsa = fertiliser.

WEDNESDAY, 27TH JANUARY, 1954

He was a soldier in the good old days;
Today I saw him lowered into the grave
Not young nor old – it's he that once was brave.
The Last Post sounded sears the cords of heart,
Six men, six shots, and three, and we depart;
Dear John Enright now lies with Ireland's dead
He was a soldier! All that now is said.

THURSDAY, 28TH JANUARY, 1954

Dawn breaks fast and fast falls the snowy flake,
God spreads this pall on earth immaculate.
On to Ballyduff I cycle through the snow,
Home in funeral of Mrs P. I go.

FRIDAY, 29TH JANUARY, 1954

This morning cobwebs hang around my brain;
Chunks, snow and ice opaque each window pane,
The Arctic spreads her circle lower and lower
With frozen teeth she's biting to the core.
Funeral today of beloved Mrs P.
She lies now in the sand beside the sea;
The monotone of the unceasing wave
Sighs 'Pace eternum' above her grave;
She was the dearest Lady of the land,
Oh! death is cruel – but then – at God's command.

Saturday, 30th January, 1954

King Frost still crushes with his iron heel;
Not easy walk the roads on even keel,
Elligott calls – Drill Motor out of gear,
Liam of course electronic engineer,
He's working hard to put the gadget right;
Shellac he paints and puts the tape on tight,
We build another flag out in the stall;
'Tis freezing like the devil over all,
This evening how I hug the kitchen range;
Just painted Shep with oil – he has the mange!

Sunday, 31st January, 1954

I read the Sunday papers after Mass –
Frost still a florist on the window glass –
Attie and Mary call from Bally B.
Grand-daughter too, a little darling she.
Her eyes dancing – blue as April skies –
Laughs all through the day and never cries,
The little Angel of their house and heart,
As new joys brighten as the old depart.
I hate this damned old doggerel rhyme,
This diary stops if I can't soar sublime.

MONDAY, 1ST FEBRUARY, 1954

Again today down from the frigid zone
The cold North-Easter freezes to the bone.
The snow lies lightly on the fields today
Oh for a thaw to see it melt away!
The skies are bright and blue as indigo
Which augurs well, more frost is 'on the go'.
I went to Bally L. and bought a car,
A second-hand – uncrocked – yet not a star;
Ere I grow senile it will suit me now,
As ageing wrinkles deepen on my brow.
I think I will retire unto my room
And seek the comfort of an Eiderdown.

TUESDAY, 2ND FEBRUARY, 1954

Ne'er before did I see Aurora leap
From such a bed of flame – never so deep
A crimson fire the sun before did wear;
It must have scorched beloved Aurora's hair!
The chicks pick up their Pin-head all in song;
All are 'Johnny Walkers'; still going strong.
Liam renovates the 'Renault' in the stall,
Her engine needs a little overhaul.
Morning's tragic news – Hindoos too anxious –
Faith fanatic, bathing in the Ganges –
A crazy ritual that thus has bound them.

THURSDAY, 4TH FEBRUARY, 1954

As looking out the window after dawn,
A large brown hare was grazing on the lawn;
He seemed to know the absence of the hound,
I watched him grazing and he gazing round;
He sleeps each day our fir-grove within,
Untroubled of this weary world's din –
Although the morning air keen and raw,
We thank the Lord – at last has come the thaw.
And all the birds are happy now to feel
The worms arise to give the morning meal.
I forged the irons for the flags in stall,
Did some chores around and that was all!

FRIDAY, 5TH FEBRUARY, 1954

The longed-for thaw has been so far maintained,
No one grouses when the day has rained;
Rain-clouds so soft – oh, what a grand exchange!
From gosh-dang frost that makes one hug the range.
Another flag we build within the stall,
To release the last heifer from the wall.
Next – reading down the paper I have seen
Our Pope (the greatest that has ever been),
Is very ill – we pray God will sustain
Him back to health and vigour once again.

SATURDAY, 6TH FEBRUARY, 1954

A case in court before Barra O'Brien,
So much upsetting that I cannot rhyme.
Compressor sold must be returned again;
Refunding money grieves – I am to blame.

SUNDAY, 7TH FEBRUARY, 1954

To Mass and home – the usual Sabbath day,
The Sunday papers pass the time away:
Today there will be no further rhyme,
I'm sick and tired and go to bed at nine.

MONDAY, 8TH FEBRUARY, 1954

Byers and Hogan call to chat with Liam;
Dialogue of course 'Vacmaster' theme.
Ten notes are mine for worthy ballad made
To fit machine and theme for their crusade –
Poor old Denis Foley has just passed on
The way the generations all have gone.
At eighty-one it ever seems to me
One's surely ripe for that eternity;
'God rest his soul' is thus our fervent prayer
Now that he's gone where the eternal are.

TUESDAY, 9TH FEBRUARY, 1954

Morning; blackbirds and thrushes start to sing;
These the first tellers of the lovely Spring.
Their first notes recall the Springs of long ago
Which I remember well – now I must go
To follow slowly Denis down to Gale,
Benumbered with his own – their dust entail –
I drink two pints at Nolan's on return
And leave the mourners who no longer mourn.
But such is life that must end up in death;
We're but remembered to our latest breath.

WEDNESDAY, 10TH FEBRUARY, 1954

There is no doubt but Spring is in the air;
The rooks now call to have a look upstair
One nest I think is all that has remained;
These subtle architects with plans unframed,
Soon will they start their noisy housing scheme;
Their nigger love begins – their Love's young Dream.
I now must start my ballad on the 'Vac'.
Win or lose I will hit along the track.
I need not climb Olympus for a song
But keep to Earth where 'dusty' themes belong.

Thursday, 11th February, 1954

Anniversary of Lourdes Apparitions

I rose this morning early, had a shave,
And soon my thoughts co-mingled with the 'Gave',
That lonely river beneath the Pyrenees
Rolling gently to the Western seas.
For on it stands the Virgin's wondrous shrine –
Lourdes! – the Grotto! – the miracles divine!
Here, in all the beauty of her heavenly state
She did proclaim herself Immaculate
To Bernadette, the poor ambassador,
Whom, too, we often pray and oft implore.

Friday, 12th February, 1954

Today they're almost ope' – the Daffodil
Out in the lawn – mid bushes on the hill,
Another day their drooping cups of gold
So beautiful and lovely to behold.
(Like shining armies buckled in array
For battle) will spread for Spring's display.
Harbingers! ye bear a message for the trees,
Ye tell the birds of song, of marriage days,
Who'll choir the morning in their ecstasies.
Ye tell the sophist rook brook no delays
But thither go and call his dusky mate
To mend their wicker home ere it be late.

146

SATURDAY, 13TH FEBRUARY, 1954

At night my feet get swollen – know not why,
Perhaps it is that I must soon now die.
If this is ominous, so to me 'twould seem
'Tis getting threadbare, this old tired machine!
And then there is one place I'd like to lie;
Near that old tower* where stream is running by;
There sweetly rippling it will ever keep
Me company there listening while I sleep.
Howe'er if hour-glass sands are running low,
Who can avert the time one has to go?

*Tower = Lisselton Graveyard.

SUNDAY, 14TH FEBRUARY, 1954

A week has passed, another week begun,
Motored down to Mass – home to lunch for one,
I gave my usual call to Cantillon's Bar
To smile and smoke and chat above our 'jar'.
Day is soft and beautiful – sun shines bright,
All nature is awaking with the light –
The rising light, Spring Equinox, is near
Matin of the birds – sweetest of the year.

MONDAY, 15TH FEBRUARY, 1954

While dancers of the Sunday night sleep sound;
I must arise and get things moving round,
I set the fire and get the kettle on;
Then get the tea-pot when 'tis on the song.
Yes! Morpheus still holds my sons in sleep;
I call in vain for still they slumber deep,
I drink a mug of tay – out to the stall –
I curse the dance hall – or I curse them all.
Day passes on with nothing to disclose,
Ah! need I say that all my sons arose!

TUESDAY, 16TH FEBRUARY, 1954

To Dr H. with Mum to Bally B.
Oh, the glory of the entrancing sea,
There is a change, I am another being,
Speaking to God, always unseen yet seeing,
Yes, seeing Him in the sands along the shore;
In cliffs that hold His waves forever more,
They too have voices like the heaving sea,
Interpretations of Eternity:
Here His Omnipresence is revealed
More than by mountain, forest, glen or field –
Home dreaming of another lovely day –
Gives joy to life, if only it would stay.

WEDNESDAY, 17TH FEBRUARY, 1954

I jumped from bed this morning with the dawn
Serene and soft – the stillness and the calm
Of this most glorious morning should inspire
And wake the Muse to new poetic fire.
I feel like Wordsworth (nature's greatest seer)
For all his golden daffodils are here.
Oh, yes, 'they flash upon the inward eye,
Which is the bliss of' – (In God's name how try
To fit the word 'of solitude' up here
With ducks a-quack and geese and crows I fear).

THURSDAY, 18TH FEBRUARY, 1954

'Tis joy to see a hare jump from its form;
'Tis joy to catch the ray of Spring's fresh morn,
Zephyrs soft blowing in from ocean deep
To kiss young Spring's soft mouth opening from
      sleep.
Again do I recall those halcyon days
The vim of youth, and Love's inconstant phase;
As last night's moon rolling up the sky
Garment clouds eclipse – soon from shadow fly.
Farmers should not be so sentimental –
For cows, calves and pigs 'tis detrimental.

WEDNESDAY, 24TH FEBRUARY, 1954

Oh, yes, I've reached the Autumn of my days
And Winter of old age creeps slowly on;
With misty eyes oft I walk the lonely ways,
For those who made life's Summer – all are gone.
Still, though life's charmed dreams remain behind,
Casket of deep joys the days still hold.
Oft will I search the archives of the mind
For poems whose cadence charms as of old,
Every year the joy of Spring will wake
My heart to ecstasy. Unsullied, true,
Old friendships richer for past sorrow's sake
Comfort my spirit as when life was new;
Though Youth's green April fade to brown and sere,
Earth still is lovely and my friends still dear.

THE BOLANDS OF FARNASTACK

The Bolands of Farnastack came from Ballynote, just east of Kilrush in County Clare. The first Boland to come to Farnastack was Patrick Boland who was born in Ballynote in 1809 and died in Ballylongford on 16 March, 1868.

It is possible that a branch of the Bolands moved from Ennis to West Clare some time in the early or middle eighteenth century. The first recorded reference to the Ballynote Bolands is in the Index to Administration Bonds for the Diocese of Killaloe in the National Archives which records that 'Patrick Boland, Ballynote, farmer' died in 1802. Patrick died intestate and it appears from the Tithe Applotment books for the Parish of Kilrush dated 23 December, 1826, that his farm of 68 acres was divided almost equally between his five sons – Daniel, Patrick, Anthony, James and Francis.

Daniel, born in 1777, was the father of Patrick of Farnastack. Daniel was a farmer and salmon fisherman. He was the occupier of 13.5 acres of land in 1826. By the time of Griffith's Primary Valuation of County Clare in 1855, he was the occupier of 31.5 acres as well as a salmon fishery. Daniel died at Ballynote on 18 April, 1867, aged 90. His wife Margaret, nee Scanlan of Doonaha, died on 24 January, 1871, aged 86.

Daniel's son Patrick (of Farnastack) became a corn merchant in Kilrush, traded in West Clare and North Kerry, had a cargo boat and engaged in the corn export trade. He was a frequent visitor to Ballylongford in the course of his business. On 19 February, 1844, at Ballylongford, he married Sarah Langan, daughter of John Langan and Honora McEvoy who farmed at Reenturk.

Sarah was born in 1822 at the Langan home at Kil-padogue beside Tarbert, where a Langan family still resides.

The Langans were cousins of the well-known poets, Micheál Ó Longáin and his son Micheál Óg, and of Tom Langan, the 1798 activist. Both Micheál Óg and Tom (who were first cousins) were United Irishmen. Tom 'Captain Steel' was the United Irishmen organiser for West Limerick and North Kerry.

Patrick and Sarah settled down in Ballylongford where he acquired a considerable amount of property. They first lived in the house in Main Street, subsequent-ly the home of Tim Kennelly. He acquired stores and offices and, for a period, rented the 'Big Store'. His corn and business declined during the famine years and even-tually it ceased. He was most charitable to the local com-munity during the famine.

By Deed dated 24 July, 1851, in which he is described as a 'shopkeeper', Patrick Boland acquired the lease of the corner house in Ballylongford (which was my child-hood home – now owned by Alan Kennelly, a great-grandson of Patrick).

Patrick turned to farming in the middle to late 1850s. First of all, he acquired the tenancy of a 31 acre farm at Lislaughtin, Ballylongford, from James Crosbie of Bally-heigue Castle. In 1858 he acquired a 31 year lease of a house and farm at Ballyline, Ballylongford, from St John Thomas Blacker and, finally on 17 September, 1858, he acquired a 31 year lease, also from St John Thomas Black-er, of the farm at Farnastack, Lisselton, consisting of the entire townland of 368 acres.

Patrick Boland and Sarah continued to reside mainly at their home in Ballylongford after acquiring Farnastack. They had seven children, all born in Ballylongford.

The eldest, Patrick, born in March, 1847, was a medical student at Queen's College, Cork, during which he wrote *Boland's Duidín* (he carved his pipe and name into the date-stone of the great barn at Farnastack), suffered ill-health and died at Farnastack on 24 July, 1875.

Catherine, born in March, 1850, married John D. Leahy of Glenduff, County Limerick, at Ballylongford on 4 February, 1869, got the Ballyline and Lislaughtin farms and the two houses adjoining the main house at Ballylongford as her dowry, had a large family and died at Limerick on 9 May, 1901. All the children emigrated to the United States where their descendants still live.

Margaret, born *c.* 1853, married Thomas Scanlon, of Newtownsandes in 1875. They ran a grocery shop in the Boland house at Ballylongford (the family had moved to Farnastack by then), was deserted by her husband and with her surviving children emigrated to the United States about 1890.

John, born in 1856, married Bridget Scanlon of Ballymackessey, Ballylongford, on 28 February, 1884 (following which he got control of Farnastack). He was very active in public affairs, was a member of Listowel Board of Guardians from 1896 to 1920 (Vice-Chairman from 1900–1906), a member of Listowel Rural District Council from 1907–1920 and a member of Kerry County Council from 1914–1920. He was made a Justice of the Peace in 1906. He died at Farnastack on 6 April, 1941. He was the father of Bob, the poet.

Their daughter Sarah married a Scanlon and they emigrated to Australia, where they both died young (about 1884).

Marianne, born September, 1859, married Con Kennelly of Pallas, Lixnaw and in 1898 got 204 acres of the Farnastack farm as her dowry. This is now owned by her grandson, Con Nolan. Con is the son of Marianne's daughter Johanna (Josie) who married Jack Nolan of Carruerragh and Tullahinell. The poet Brendan Kennelly is another grandson of Marianne. Marianne died on 10 June, 1954.

Daniel, the youngest child, was born in May, 1862, married Nonie Gunn, lived at Lyre, emigrated with her to the United States, returned after some time, got part of the Gunn farm and became an auctioneer. He died suddenly in 1928. They had one son, Daniel, who died in 1946.

Patrick Boland Senior died at his house in Ballylongford on 16 March, 1868, aged 59 years. By his Will dated 27 December, 1867, he bequested all his property to his wife Sarah 'in Trust and management for all my children'.

The family appear to have moved more or less permanently to Farnastack – to the 'Steward's House' – shortly after Patrick's death. The house at Ballylongford (the corner house) was let to the Parish Priest, Michael O'Sullivan, from 1870 to 1875 when the new presbytery and church at Ballylongford were presumably completed. Previously the Parish Priest resided in Asdee. The house was subsequently occupied by Thomas Scanlon, who was married to Margaret Boland, as mentioned earlier. John Boland is recorded as the occupier from 1892 to 1897.

Sarah Boland ruled Farnastack with a firm hand. Known to all as 'Ma' Boland, she was a most able head of family. She built a substantial new house in 1872/73 – to become known as Farnastack House – and completed the great barn in 1874. Her building work represented a farmstead on a grand scale and survives virtually intact to this day. Each morning she spaced out the work to be completed by workmen for the day. She died at Farnastack on 6 April, 1897, aged 75.

By Deed of Assignment dated 8 January, 1881, Farnastack was assigned to Trustees in trust on the conditions set out in the Will of Patrick Boland. Following his marriage in 1884, as already mentioned, John Boland, the elder surviving son, was given control of Farnastack by the Trustees. The lease of Farnastack expired on 16 September, 1889. On 31 October, 1889, St John Thomas Blacker-Douglas and John Boland signed a Fair Rent Agreement under the Land Law (Ireland) Act, 1881, wherein they agreed a rent of £100 a year for the lands of Farnastack. St John Thomas died on 26 February, 1900, and was succeeded by his eldest son, Maxwell Vandeleur Blacker-Douglas. On 1 November 1905, Maxwell Vandeleur and the tenants, John Boland and his sister Marianne Kennelly, signed a Purchase Agreement under the Irish Land Act, 1903, providing for the purchase by John and Marianne of their respective parts of the lands of Farnastack.

John Boland and Bridget, parents of the poet, had the following children:

Patrick (Attie – my father), born at Ballylongford on 20 January 1885, died on 21 April, 1922;

Sarah Mary Angela (Ciss), born at Farnastack on 13 September, 1886, married Patrick McNamara, died on 24 December, 1955;

Michael Valentine (Bob – a childhood name – self-styled facetiously on occasion as Robert Leslie Boland, Bart., the subject of this book), born at Farnastack on 14 February, 1888, inherited Farnastack (other than Marianne's part), died on 17th November, 1955;

Daniel, born at Farnastack on 1 January, 1891, died on 28 June, 1973;

Male infant born at Farnastack on 9 January, 1893, survived only 20 hours;

Honora (Norrie), born at Ballylongford on 22 June, 1895, married Dr. Patrick O'Grady, died on 2 December 1976;

John (Jackie), born at Farnastack on 25 August, 1898, died on 5 January, 1958 (father of Most Reverend Raymond Boland, consecrated Bishop of Birmingham, Alabama on 25 March, 1988).

Michael Valentine (Bob) sold some of the Farnastack lands and later divided the remaining between his sons, Dan and Bernard. The latter's part included Farnastack House. Following Bernard's death, intestate, on 7 November, 1987, his property was acquired by his nephew Joseph Boland (son of Dan), who is the present owner.

JOSEPH BOLAND, POET'S NEPHEW

MOLONEY UP AND AT IT

Brendan Kennelly

Moloney Up and At It is a collection of comic poems with a central character, Moloney, who tells of his experiences of, for the most part, sex and death. The language of the poems is that of the south-west of Ireland, of north Kerry in particular. Brendan Kennelly captures the easy, bawdy humour, the candid speech and the fluent narrative power of the men and women he heard telling stories of this kind.

LOVE OF IRELAND
POEMS OF THE IRISH

Brendan Kennelly

Love of Ireland is a magical collection of translations from the Irish by one of Ireland's leading poets, Brendan Kennelly. Here he has captured all of the sponaneity, candour, freshness and emotional fullness of Irish poetry.

A HIGH MEADOW

John B. Keane

Mollie's face clouded as it always did whenever she thought of the Ram of God. She was careful not to show her annoyance. The more she considered their relationship the more her fury mounted. She was always fond of saying that there was a fly in every ointment no matter how settled the scene. There was always one hitch and the Ram of God was hers. Somehow, in the course of time, she would bring him down. There was no doubt whatsoever about that in her mind. She would use the man by her side and his powerful connections, unknown to either, but use them she would in the pursuance of her steely determination to ruin the one man who had so far proved to be invincible as far as Mollie was concerned. She would find a way. She tried in vain to subjugate the intense annoyance which the mention of his name always seemed to stimulate ... 'I'll even the score with the Ram of God and he'll rue the day he crossed swords with Mollie Cronane.'

BALLADS OF A BOGMAN

Sigerson Clifford

Almost invariably Sigerson Clifford has set his word pictures against the mountain backdrop that edges Dingle Bay from the Laune to the Inney. To visit his Kerry is to go with him along the heathery pathways above Cahirciveen, or to sit with him in the cosy pub at The Point while the long ferryboat noses out from The Island. With a rare sense of imtimacy he will take you, on bare feet through the dew-wet grass of sloping fields before the morning sun tops the shoulder of one of his mountains, or set you down in the scent of smouldering turf under low rafters as darkly brown as the stout in your glass. In these ballads Sigerson Clifford has caught and held the witchery of Kerry.

FAVOURITE POEMS WE LEARNED IN SCHOOL

Thomas F. Walsh

Thomas F. Walsh has put together a collection of the most quoted and most memorable poems we learned in school. The poems in this anthology will remain with us until we reach the end of our journey in this life, mainly because we learned them when we were young, and consequently they have become part of us.